SECRETS OF CHAMPIONSHIP KARATE

KARYN TURNER
with Mark Van Schuyver

CB
CONTEMPORARY
BOOKS
CHICAGO

Library of Congress Cataloging-in-Publication Data

Turner, Karyn.
    Secrets of championship karate / Karyn Turner with Mark Van
Schuyver.
        p.   cm.
    Includes index.
    ISBN 0-8092-4052-1
    1. Karate.   I. Schuyver, Mark Van.   II. Title.
GV1114.3.T87   1991
796.8'153—dc20   90-28463
                                               CIP

Interior photos by James Baca,
by Frank Simon, and from the
personal collection of Karyn Turner

Published by Contemporary Books, Inc.
180 North Michigan Avenue, Chicago, Illinois 60601
Manufactured in the United States of America
International Standard Book Number: 0-8092-4052-1

To Aldean, Don, Gary, Billye, Donna, and J.C.

Contents

Foreword

I have read many books on karate and karate technique, but never before have I encountered a volume like *Secrets of Championship Karate*. There are hundreds of karate books on the market that teach everything from strategy to stances, but this is the first one that teaches everything you need to know to become a karate champion.

Karyn Turner knows the martial arts from the inside and the outside. She is a champion of fighting and forms, a promoter of champions, and a trainer of champions. She knows every trick in the karate universe, and she shares them all in this book.

When Karyn Turner and Mark Van Schuyver first told me about *Secrets of Championship Karate*, I expected a book for beginners. Yet there is material here that only a handful of karate competitors has ever seen. Through her interpretations of Bruce Lee's principles of winning, Karyn presents an unstoppable formula for tournament success.

Whether you are a beginner or an old pro, you will learn much from *Secrets of Championship Karate*.

Bill Wallace

Acknowledgments

Thanks to my son Gary, who always had to explain to his friends why his mother was working out on a speed bag while their mothers were baking cookies; to my family, for being my biggest fan and for instilling in me the belief you can become what you dream; to Al Dacascos, who taught me the spirit and truth of martial arts; to Howard Jackson, for never letting me quit; to Lena Miller, for being my friend and giving me the time to write; and to Mark Van Schuyver, who shaped my ideas and experiences into this book.

Thanks to Bill Wallace, Jim Butin, Aboe Hada, Dan Inosanto, Thurman Karan, Jeri Van Cook, Fred Wren, Jim Harrison, Jhoone Rhee, and Howard Jackson for the interviews.

Thanks to Linda Lee, Joe Lewis, Chuck Norris, Steve Fisher, John Natividad, Skipper Mullins, Kenny Street, John Worley, Ed Parker, Jeff Smith, Chuck Martinez, Benny Urquidez, John Corcoran, Mike Stone, Hidy Ochiai, Bruce Lee, Eric Lee, and The Hard Knocks. Very special thanks to Bill Wallace, for his many contributions to the project.

Self-expression is the element that brings the crowd to its feet. Here Turner demonstrates her unique slicing moves performed with Chinese broad swords.

1
The Elements
of Victory

The crowd exploded with emotion. Screams and cheers echoed from the rafters. My body moved into a spontaneous attack. My opponent tried to cover—too late. I earned a solid point as I slammed yet another spinning backkick into the tall woman's midsection.

"Point!" the referee shouted.

We clashed again, and a left hook slipped through my guard. Sparks filled my eyes and a flash of pain erupted in my temple—a point lost. I bit down on my mouthpiece and hid the pain as I had been taught to do.

From the line I faded to the left and at the same instant launched a roundhouse. First I felt, then heard, the impact of my kick as it crunched into her ribs. Point.

In a fury she chased me with a frontkick and a barrage of punches. I deflected the kick and her jabs. Against my defenses her powerful reverse punches rained harmlessly. She whirled. Spray hit my face and hands as I ducked her spinning hookkick. No point lost.

I threw a frontkick/backfist combination, but she managed to evade. From the corner of my eye I caught the blur of another hook coming in on my right. I slipped the punch and folded the big woman in half with a left uppercut to the solar plexus. Our foreheads collided

1

After faking a kick, Karyn Turner (right) scores with a punch.

in an accidental crash, and we both reeled away from the stun. A point hard won.

The referee's voice was drowned out by the shouting and screaming of the Texas crowd. I faked with my shoulder and then launched myself forward with a skipping sidekick. My foot thudded home. The big woman stumbled backward, nearly falling.

"Break," the referee barked. The match was over, the points well in my favor.

Never taking my eyes off my opponent, I returned to the line. The breath was hot in my lungs, but the spring was still in my step. It was the final fight in a long day of forms and fighting.

Then came the announcement: "Karyn Turner, winner and still champion." I felt a great sense of fulfillment. The sweat and work of countless hours of training and preparation had paid off again.

For me, nothing equals the emotion, the excitement, and the tremendous satisfaction that comes from being a true and consistent karate champion. The feeling is like falling in love; it is a thrill that must be experienced to be fully understood.

But there is more to tournament competition than just the joy of winning and the recognition that comes from being a champion. Through competition I learned more about myself than I ever dreamed I would know. I changed and grew as an individual. After a few years on the tournament circuit, I became ten times the martial artist that I was when I started, and my self-confidence increased fivefold.

You do not need buckets of natural ability to become a top-rated point karate competitor. Most of us who have achieved this goal were blessed in the beginning with nothing more than average ability and a whole lot of "want to."

If you are filled with a desire to be the best, and if you are willing to apply the techniques for winning that you are about to learn, nothing can stop you from winning trophy after trophy, tournament after tournament. You too can become a karate champion.

Turner holding her trophies from Ed Parker's Internationals Tournament.

The Art of War

Like many first-time competitors I made my fighting debut with a flurry of flowery movements and untested techniques. I was dismayed to discover that many of my techniques lacked power, and most of my well-planned strategies did not work. Quickly I was forced to realize that my imagined skill level was far above my actual skill level. It was a painful but important lesson. Consider the words of Sun Tzu in the ancient Chinese book *The Art of War*: "Know your enemy and know yourself and you will fight a hundred battles without disaster. When you are ignorant of the enemy but know yourself, your chances of winning or losing are equal. If ignorant both of your enemy and of yourself, you are certain in every battle to be in peril. . . ." In tournament competition we come face to face with our own weaknesses and strengths. We "meet" ourselves in addition to meeting our opponents. We learn the truth about combat, the same harsh truth that prevails on the street as well as in the tournament circuit.

Sport karate's greatest goal is not the destruction of your opponent but rather the discovery of your self. In my career I faced hundreds of opponents, each one a new challenge against whom I tested my abilities as I widened my understanding of combat and competition.

It's Just You Out There

Like most beginners I tended to place the blame elsewhere when I lost—on the judges, coaches, referees, rules, or weather conditions. Anyone and anything seemed a good scapegoat for my failures. It took a bitter fight against a savvy opponent to awaken me to the fact that I alone was responsible for what I did or did not accomplish.

This particular event, held in Fort Worth and sponsored by Pat Burlson, was a national competition and an important stop on the tournament circuit. There were two divisions at that time, light and heavy. As always I weighed in at 126 pounds. Anyone over 125 pounds had to fight heavyweight.

My opponent was much larger than I and had far greater reach. Her size alone did not intimidate me, but when she walked across the line, looked me squarely in the eye, and said, "I am going to knock that bun right off of your head," I was dumbfounded. Anger flooded through me in hot waves. I went to the line enraged.

From the start it was a brawl. I forgot the 18 Principles of Winning (discussed later in this chapter) and I forgot my strategy. I ignored

At home, Turner shows off a few of her trophies.

advice shouted from my coach, Al Dacascos. I forgot everything except my furor.

She had made me so angry that I tried to fight her toe-to-toe even though she outweighed me by 35 pounds. I became further enraged when she finally beat me.

I reflected on my performance for many hours. It might have been days before I realized that it was my own rage that had defeated me. By letting her infuriate me, I gave her the edge she needed. I fought in anger and I lost from anger. She got me to fight her fight and she won. I understood too late that if only I had applied what I knew with a cool head I could easily have beaten that woman.

There was no one to point the finger at except me. That's when I got the real picture; there had never been and never would be anyone to blame for my failure except me.

Adaptability

To win you must be aware that martial competition is an ever-changing interaction between contestants, judges, spectators, and referees. Unlike daily karate training, competition is never static. A fight is very much alive. Fighting in the street without rules and fighting in a karate match with carefully regulated procedures are both combat, and combat is never fixed.

Changes come quickly in tournaments. Our opponents, the bias of the judges, and the conditions for performing our *kata* (a choreographed sequence of martial arts techniques), are all subject to change. From the constant challenge of change we learn adaptability.

Each fight is unique and each fighter is unique. Because of combat's fluid and unpredictable nature, you must compete frequently in order to be victorious against many different fighters who have a variety of fight styles.

The Reality of Karate

Spiritual concepts and mental aspirations are greatly overemphasized in many martial arts schools. Students too often see these things as

Turner walks the ring after a demonstration at the Las Vegas Hilton for ABC television.

reasons for not testing themselves in competition. Do not use this cop-out. Nothing can substitute for the lessons of competition.

The secrets of karate remain secrets until we discover them for ourselves through practice and martial competition. For me, competition is the reality of karate. It is the quickest and clearest pathway to the ancient wisdom of the Oriental martial arts. The true value of your karate technique evolves from the awareness you gain in tournament competition. Win or lose, you'll always gain from the tournament experience.

The Mechanical Stage

All champion martial artists have mastered the basics. When they set out on the long road to their titles, they began by learning the mechanics of karate technique. There are no shortcuts to mechanical skill.

Despite my solid technical skill, however, I was inconsistent at winning tournaments. When I did win, the victory was often by a spread of only one point. My scores in kata were no better.

After many contests I came to understand that good karate technique alone is not enough to build a championship record. Self-expression was missing from my performances.

Self-Expression

One of the primary purposes of competition karate or any art form is self-expression. Where winning is concerned, self-expression in forms and fighting is a critical factor. Self-expression fills your performance with depth and beauty—and it is the element that brings the crowd to its feet.

There is a systematic, mechanical method of karate technique training, but in competition there is no such method of application. In the classroom a kick is a kick and a punch is a punch, but in a tournament you must "discover" the technique, *i.e.*, find the full versatility of the technique as it applies to combat. Through creative self-expression in combat you use your techniques in a variety of ways. You find out if, and how, they can work for you.

Self-expression also gives you vitality and the charisma victors have. It is the essence of the martial arts. It is your reason for putting your skill on the line and for being there in front of all those people.

Winning with Self-Expression

After I began to win consistently in the women's category for kata, I decided to step up into the men's division, where the rivalry for first place was much keener. For a long time I lost as many contests as I won.

My breakthrough finally came in a national competition in the men's black belt division. Because I was scheduled to be one of the last contestants to demonstrate, I could study the performances of the majority of the other contestants. I observed that most of them and all of the judges were hard stylists (practitioners of systems that rely on extreme tension and brute power—hard blows with maximum power).

The kata I had prepared for this event was built mostly of soft-style Chinese kung fu techniques. I realized that these hard-style judges would be especially biased against this soft and flowing kata. So, in the last minutes before I was to perform, I decided to change things around.

My new plan was to open my kata with crisp, hard techniques, and then vary the rhythm of my softer Chinese-style movements to emphasize their hidden power. For a close, I decided to execute one of my most solid hard-style movements. I imagined that my performance would be like a song: chorus, verse, chorus.

I knew that what I was about to do was risky. It is dangerous to change things at the last minute. Still I felt certain that I was on the right track. I experienced a great rush of energy as I anticipated my performance.

One big problem still remained. The judges who had already observed the better part of twenty excellent competitors must surely be falling asleep. How to get their attention?

When it was my turn to perform, I walked to the end of the ring. On a whim I did a triple butterfly kick. This was highly unusual, and they must have thought I was crazy. But I had their full attention when I introduced myself and set my form in motion.

I felt my form come alive. I hit highs and lows with a grace and power I had never known before. My kata became more than just a sequence of techniques. The pattern evolved beyond the boundaries of preformed kata to become a living thing—a creation rather than just a re-creation. The kata was an expression of my inner self.

To the cheers of the crowd I ended my form with a solid hard-style technique. The performance was my best ever. My kata and my form seemed to transcend the mechanical actions of karate and became for

Turner poses with her first-place trophy after her win in a men's black-belt kata division.

the first time martial "art." The judges awarded me the first-place trophy.

In every tournament from that day forward I expressed myself in much the same way. My winnings increased, and never again did I fear competition against men in kata.

Finally my dream of being a champion was within sight. Only one important step remained; I had to fully master the 18 Principles of Winning.

Karyn Turner's Interpretation of Bruce Lee's Principles of Winning

All the best *karateka* train hard. The elite competitors have solid basics and the ability to express themselves creatively. But the big champions—the megastars like Bill Wallace, Chuck Norris, Howard Jackson, Joe Lewis, Benny ("the Jet") Urquidez, and Jeff Smith—also apply what can be called the universal principles of winning to everything they do.

Just as the sculptor creates a statue not by adding rock but rather by hacking away the unessential stone until the creative vision is uncovered, the champion karateka uses the principles of winning to tear away at the competition until, as Bruce Lee believed, the truth is exposed.

Theoretically, all of the principles can be used with any single technique. A fighter may, therefore, choose one maneuver, such as a roundkick, and apply the winning principles to it in a variety of combinations to make it act like dozens of different fighting techniques.

The 18 Principles and the Two Realities that follow have evolved from the works of the late Bruce Lee. Before and after his death these principles were passed down in several versions. The most complete version that I have seen and the one on which I have based my own fighting strategy was given to me by his widow, Linda.

Many champions owe their success to some or all of these universal concepts for winning. In later chapters you will learn to apply the 18 Principles of Winning to your favorite techniques and to your tournament strategy.

The 18 Principles of Winning

1. The Principle of Setups

A. Set yourself up to win both mentally and physically through rigorous physical and mental training.
B. Set up your opponent with verbal and nonverbal communications.
C. Set up the judges and referee by exhibiting the attitude of a winner.

Many battles are won without the firing of a single bullet. So it is with karate tournaments. You can beat your opponent before you ever lay a fist on him if you apply the theory of setups. With the Principle of Setups working for you, judges and referees will lean toward you on every decision.

2. The Principle of Positioning

A. Position yourself for mobility.
B. Position yourself for the best defensive capability.

C. Position yourself for the best offensive capability.

D. Position yourself with the right psychological attitude.

Superior position is gained through the use of footwork, angles of attack, and broken rhythm. By understanding the theory of positioning you can get inside your opponent's defenses and attack him with impunity. With a thorough grasp of this principle you will fight with maximum effectiveness from a highly protected position.

In tournament fighting a strong defense is a strong offense. By maintaining superior defensive structure and positioning, you can simultaneously attack and defend, thereby rendering your opponent helpless.

3. The Principle of Independent Movement

A. Make all movement independent.

B. Do not telegraph your intent.

C. Avoid premeditated combinations.

With independent movement, each technique happens as it needs to happen. Independent movement is a reaction to opportunity rather than a prediction of possible opportunities. The theory of independent movement means moving spontaneously without forethought and without telegraphing your intent.

4. The Principle of Initial Speed

A. Explode into your leading offensive technique.

B. Explode into your defensive techniques.

C. Push off to gain maximum speed and penetration with your opening techniques.

Howard Jackson applied the Principle of Initial Speed with unparalleled effectiveness. From the line he would explode into his opponent with such speed that he frequently got his point before his opponent could make a move to defend.

Once I saw Howard score by using initial speed three times in quick succession against a top veteran fighter. Each time he flew forward and struck before the man could move. So frustrated was his opponent after losing the third point that the man threw his black belt on the floor and walked out.

During a fight Howard Jackson exploded into his opponent with such speed that he frequently got his point before his opponent could make a move to defend.

Howard Jackson's ability to use the Principle of Initial Speed is one of the reasons he is in the job he has today. He is employed as Chuck Norris's bodyguard.

5. The Principle of Attack Lines

A. Attack your opponent along his inside line.
B. Attack your opponent on his middle line.
C. Attack your opponent along his line.

These lines are the pathways to your opponent's vulnerable zones. The Principle of Attack Lines guides and directs every punch you throw and every kick you deliver. By applying this theory you will land more blows and parry more punches than you ever dreamed possible.

6. The Principle of Bridging the Gap

A. Use certain methods to advance into striking range.
B. Advance to the point at which you are able to kick your opponent.
C. Advance to the point at which you are able to punch your opponent.

The gap is the dead space between you and your opponent. It is the neutral zone in which neither fighter can reach the other. To win you must bridge this distance with footwork, hyperextension, double hyperextension, faking, and other techniques to get within striking distance.

7. The Principle of Simplicity of Technique

A. Pick three to five techniques and learn them well.
B. Avoid fancy, difficult techniques.
C. Rely on the basics and apply the principles.

When we first begin training we are taught the basics. Once we have a handle on them, we learn tough moves that few people can do well, such as butterfly kicks and axe kicks, and other beautiful and complex moves. But there is little room for such finery in a fight or a tournament. The last thing you would throw in the street is one of these fancy and difficult techniques.

In a fight you must cut away all of the flowery stuff you may have learned in karate. In a tournament the primary techniques, such as the backfist, inverted punch, the side-, round-, and backkick, work best. You do not even need to use all of these—pick three that you like, apply the principles, and you will be a remarkably flexible contender.

Joe Lewis relied almost exclusively on three techniques: a backfist, a backkick, and a sidekick. I never saw him use anything else, yet he was a superb fighter and a top champion.

Lewis chose to use the principles with his backkick and sidekick. For me, the backfist, the reverse punch, the lead-leg sidekick, and the roundkick work best.

You too should stick to a few techniques that work well for you. Keep your art simple. Learn to apply your favorites in a myriad of ways. Change the angle of your attack rather than changing your techniques.

Champion Joe Lewis relied almost exclusively on three techniques—a backfist, a backkick, and a sidekick.

8. The Principle of Motion Economy

A. Conserve motion by using straight lines.
B. Economize motion by attacking with the closest weapon to the target.
C. Use direct angles for attack and defense.

Don't waste motion. Increase your speed and power by taking the most direct route to your target and by using techniques that waste no time.

9. The Principle of Relaxation

A. Relax your body to conserve your limited supply of energy.
B. Relax with each technique to increase your speed.
C. Relax your body to increase your power.

Relaxation is a weapon. When you apply relaxation to every technique, your speed will increase by an incredible margin. Relax your mind, and you will gain even more speed from improved reflexes.

10. The Principle of Mobility

A. Use your footwork patterns to cover distance.
   1. Basic stepping
   2. Switch stepping
   3. Shuffling
   4. Hopping
   5. Creeping
B. Apply your footwork in three directions.
   1. Vertical
   2. Horizontal
   3. Arcing
C. Do everything while your body is in motion.
   1. Strike while in motion.
   2. Defend while in motion.
   3. Fake your opponent while in motion.

Footwork patterns and directions give you the ability to move in and out of attack positions. Use footwork to advance toward, retreat from, and fake out your opponent. Like other action sports, karate is a moving game.

11. The Principle of Reach

A. Extend to the limit of your reach.
B. Hyperextend by sliding forward a bit as you execute a maneuver.
C. Double hyperextend by skipping or hopping forward and then sliding forward as you execute your technique.

The Principle of Reach is applied to a technique through footwork and body positioning. You will learn special stepping and extending drills that will enable you to "reach out and clobber someone" from a distance at which he considers himself safe.

12. The Centerline Principle

A. Attack the many targets found on your opponent's centerline.
B. Expect attack when you open your centerline.
C. Bring all your body weapons to bare by angling your centerline.

The Centerline Principle is both defensive and offensive. This theory is so important that entire martial arts systems are founded on its intricacies. Wing chun, Bruce Lee's first system, is based upon the centerline theory.

This principle has unique applications in sport karate, in which more emphasis is placed on a point gain than on the amount of power behind each hit. To keep your opponent from scoring, protect your centerline at all times with defensive hand positioning and by body angling.

Attack your opponent's centerline targets with vigor, but risk opening your center only when the opportunity for landing a cross-body technique, such as a rear-leg kick or a reverse punch, is very clear.

13. The Principle of Straight Lines

A. Gain extra power by attacking in straight lines.
B. Take the shortest route to the nearest target.
C. Gain speed by attacking with straight lines.

Straight-line attacks beat circular defenses and should make up the majority of your strikes. Such attacks are fast and extremely hard to defend against. Straight-line defensive movements defeat your opponent's attack by wedging him out of the centerline area, the shortest distance to your target.

14. The Principle of Faking

A. Fake with your hips, body, and shoulders.
B. Fake to scare your opponent into moving.
C. Fake to destroy your opponent's timing.

Fakes cause your opponent to do what you want him to do. Take advantage of his reaction, following your fakes with hard-hitting techniques.

15. The Principle of Constant Forward Pressure

A. Apply forward movement to keep your opponent on the defensive.
B. Use aggressive body language.
C. Exert constant mental pressure to keep your mind in the fight and your opponent on the run.

Constant mental and physical pressure exerted on your opponent will keep him constantly on guard.

16. The Principle of Timing

A. Attack him before he can move.
B. Attack him as he moves.
C. Attack him after he moves.

Evaluate your own and your opponent's timing. Once you have discovered his pattern, you can break the back of his offense by attacking him between the beats.

17. The Principle of Angles of Attack

A. Attack your opponent with direct angles.
B. Attack your opponent with oblique angles.
C. Attack your opponent with deceptive angles.

Attack your opponent using the angles to which he is most vulnerable and you are best protected. By understanding how triangles can be used to confuse and outmaneuver your opponent, you're on your way to scoring points on an international scale.

18. The Principle of Broken Rhythm

A. Mix up your targets and strike your opponent in low, middle, and high areas.
B. Vary the rhythm of your movements between passive and active.
C. Change the motion of your body. Mix forward and backward motions in unpredictable patterns.
D. Alternate the speed of your techniques. Mix slow and fast attacks to throw off your opponent's timing.
E. Mix faking and attacking.
F. Change your attitude from passive to aggressive.
G. Switch your line of attack from inside to outside, and back again.
H. Mix relaxation and tension to throw off your opponent.

Confuse your opponent by using broken patterns of movement and broken rhythms. Be totally unpredictable.

The Two Realities

In addition to the principles, I have isolated what I call the two realities of combat. These concepts are an extension of my interpretation of the principles, and they apply to all fighting situations.

1. The Four Types of Opponent

According to my interpretation of Lee's original principles, there are only four types of opponents: the charger, the blocker, the runner, and the elusive runner.

The charger moves forward constantly; the blocker stays in position or takes a half step back; the runner runs away mostly in a straight backward line; and the elusive runner runs and moves all over the floor in unpredictable patterns.

After determining what type of opponent you are up against, you can quickly adapt your techniques and apply the principles necessary to meet the challenge. In Chapter 3 you will learn how to identify and overcome each type.

2. Critical Distance

    A. Advance to kicking range.
    B. Advance to punching range.
    C. Understand the defensive ranges.

To hit or be hit, you must be inside the critical-distance line—that is, the battle line. It is the point at which you are close enough to reach your opponent. Next you must understand which offensive and defensive techniques and principles work best at which range.

I became a champion largely because I incorporated these principles into my style of fighting. They helped me win consistently in kata and in the fighting, not by one point but by a 3–5-point spread in whatever division I was competing.

I am not a particularly tough fighter. Many of my opponents were faster and stronger than I; yet I won victory after victory. I used the 18 Principles of Winning to build a strategy that helped me outthink and outmaneuver my competition.

The principles gave me a method and a reason for everything I did in competition. These principles provided me with the versatility I needed to stay in control in every fight and every forms competition.

One Principle Is Worth a Thousand Techniques

Among the best fighters of our time is karate superstar Bill Wallace. Early in his career Wallace suffered a knee injury that permanently impaired his right leg. To compensate for this limitation, he fought with his left side forward and kicked only with his left leg. In all the years I watched him fight I never saw him use more than three kicks: a sidekick, a roundkick, and a hookkick.

Even though he used only three kicking techniques, none of his opponents managed to get around his incredible left leg. Why? Partly because he was naturally fast but mainly because he always applied the winning principles to his kicks. His three basic techniques were transformed by these principles into dozens, perhaps hundreds, of unstoppable variations.

Bill "Superfoot" Wallace was karate's fastest kicker. He used only three kicks—a sidekick, a hookkick and a roundkick— but in unbeatable variations.

Bill Wallace never had to add techniques or change his methods. Because of his ability to apply the principles, his physical "limitation" proved to be nothing of the sort.

It is far more important to be versatile in the application of a few solid techniques than it is to learn a hundred techniques and have no understanding of the winning principles. What matters is not how much karate we know but rather how much karate we can apply.

The Principles in Action

Ed Parker's Internationals Tournament, held each year in California, is the granddaddy of all karate competitions; it is the one to win for national and international recognition. It was at the Internationals that I was forced to put the 18 Principles of Winning to their toughest test.

The Internationals comprises two days of forms and fighting. There are no rests for the 3,000 to 4,500 competitors. The black belt competition is phenomenal. Imagine an entire coliseum floor filled with twenty rings. Every division is black belt.

By the time I got to the Internationals, I had learned to apply all of the principles to my forms and fighting. Like most fighters, I had begun to specialize in certain principles. I was enjoying particularly good success with the principles of Initial Speed and Angles of Attack, using direct angles.

To get ready for the event, I spent a great deal of time working out with Howard Jackson to learn his famous initial moves. My strategy for the Internationals competition would rely heavily on the first-strike secrets I learned from Jackson.

On Saturday I took first in kata. I fought my way through the eliminations and was scheduled to fight in the finals on Sunday. Unfortunately, I got kicked in the knee during a bout. My injury was painful and my knee and leg were greatly weakened.

I had about 24 hours before the final fight to talk to myself and get ready for the battle. That 24 hours also gave the injury plenty of time to swell and become more painful. I had to concentrate more than ever on the mental aspect of the sport.

I knew who my opponent was going to be. Unhurt I was confident I had the ammunition to beat her, but with my injury I was not so sure.

I knew that my reputation was working for me. I reasoned that she was probably ready mentally. I pinned my hopes on the idea that the psychological advantage I held would compensate for my injury.

But when I walked into the circle I knew that my injury was obvious. The pain was so great that try as I might I could not keep from limping. Whatever psychological advantage I might have had was fading with each halting step.

The realization that I would surely lose overwhelmed me, and I felt resentful. Over the past months I had achieved considerable recognition in karate. Now, on the most important day of the year, at the event that could be the turning point of my career, I was nearly crippled.

Initial speed and direct attack—the principles I had relied on to get me through the eliminations—both depend on the ability to push off fast and strong. With my knee injury there was no way that I could use them. Howard Jackson's hot first-strike attacks were all dead.

Because of her greater size and weight and because of the weakness of my knee I knew that I would not be mobile enough to bridge the gap and get inside her critical-distance line. As I looked up into her eyes, I realized that I was not going to be able to use most of the other principles either. My mouth was dry with the coppery taste of fear.

What principles could I possibly use? Not mobility, hyperextension, broken rhythms, combinations, or any footwork pattern. The only remaining option I could think of was to fight a fully defensive battle. So be it. I lifted my guard.

For the first few minutes of the bout my defensive strategy worked beautifully. Despite the pain in my knee, I earned several points before she could figure out my strategy.

Then, by adjusting her timing, she was able to come in strong and trade shots with me in a quick and nearly equal exchange. It must have looked to the judges like we were just swapping blows, and because she was bigger and more aggressive, they gave her all the points.

The score was tied at 3-3, and we went to sudden death. The next point would determine the winner. My defensive strategy was no longer working. What to do?

For the sudden death the referee made us turn around and face out. At the last moment the two principles that I might still use flashed into my mind—faking and angle of attack.

I faked, hoping to make her think I was going to do the same direct defensive move that I had done before. When she rushed in, I altered my angle of defense by moving 45 degrees to the left and, bingo, I got the winning point—a reverse punch to the floating ribs.

With this win, I became the first person, male or female, to win both the forms and fighting titles simultaneously at the Internationals.

You Can Make It Happen

In the chapters that follow, you will learn how to use the 18 Principles of Winning to enhance your fighting, your form, your self-confidence, and your ability to interact and communicate with others. You will learn the rules, regulations, and procedures of the point karate circuit. In short, you will learn everything you need to know to become a karate champion.

2
Before You Compete

Long before the champion enters the arena he begins the process of winning. His thoughts are always on winning. Each day he trains his body hard, striving always for peak performance. He programs his mind, filling his head with visions of victory. For the champion, competition is a constant mind-set.

The champion's competitive spirit soars to its highest point the moment he sets foot inside the building in which a competition is being held. From that time forward every step he takes and every word he speaks is for the purpose of winning the day.

The true karate champion comes to an event ready to stomp out all comers. He is at work both inside and outside the ring. Before, during, and after each tournament, he applies the 18 Principles of Winning to make sure that victory comes his way. His weapons include much more than just his fists and feet. His mind-set, his voice, his body language, and his personality all enter into his formula for success.

With karate, as with any other worthwhile pursuit, it will take several years of hard work for you to become a top contender. You will invest countless hours in study and practice, fine-tuning your mind and body.

Apply the principles to everything you do and gradually you will

23

Turner performing a winning kata.

learn to outthink, outplan, and outperform your most talented rivals. Becoming a champion is a big job and the training is tough. If it were easy, everybody would be a karate champion.

Training for Peak Performance

Before you compete you must train your body and your mind. The training routine you choose will make you or break you, so it is important that you get a top-notch instructor, preferably one with much tournament experience who knows what the competition is doing.

Traditional karate tournaments are quite different from contact fighting sports. Some practitioners shun point karate competition believing, mistakenly, that training for a karate tournament requires the same grueling full-time schedule endured by boxers and kickboxers.

Make no mistake, you will have to train hard, but you do not have to rise before the sun, drink raw egg shakes, and run until you lose them. Let's take a look at the difference between training for a full contact match and training for the open karate tournament circuit.

Boxers and kickboxers train for each specific fight. They begin three or four months before the bout and put everything into the effort. Their goal is to build up gradually until they attain an extreme conditioning "high" that peaks out right at the time of the match. They train this way because they know that to win or even survive a boxing or kickboxing match (some of which last fifteen rounds) they must be in superb shape.

In the days following a fight the full contact fighter cools down, allowing his body to rest and his conditioning level to recede. Full contact fighters train this way because it is impossible to maintain a state of maximum conditioning.

As a traditional karate competitor your training should not be based on an extreme and stressful training routine with severe peaks and lows. You may burn yourself out completely if you attempt to maintain such a high level of physical endurance for weeks or months at a time.

Point matches are shorter and less intense than full contact matches. You will fight several opponents in one day, but you will never have to push your body to its absolute limits.

Because you will compete often you will not get long periods of rest to recover if you overtrain. You have to stay in shape all the time while avoiding overexertion.

Keeping your body at a standard level of physical conditioning does not mean that you can be lazy about your training. Point competitors are increasingly serious about their circuit. The fighters you will face today are in considerably better shape than their counterparts were ten years ago.

The requirements for point karate will probably never rival the levels of energy needed to run a 26.2-mile marathon or to compete in full contact kickboxing. But if you expect to win you will have to keep your body in above average condition.

Bill Wallace, who fought in both point and full contact karate matches, said: "In my day a fighter would light a cigarette before a match, hand the cigarette to a friend, fight the bout, and then grab the cigarette on his way out of the ring. Today fighters work out before a bout, fight, and then return to the workout room. They have combined better techniques with increased stamina."

Perfecting Your Technique

Perfecting your technique for forms and fighting is at least as important to your tournament success as is your general physical conditioning. Each day you must work hard to make each technique as perfect as it can possibly be. The perfection of your sidekick, roundkick, backfist, reverse punch, footwork patterns, and other essential techniques is your mission. The hard work and Spartan training regime will pay off when you fight and when you stand before the crowd and perform your nearly perfect kata in competition.

Thinking Like a Champion

A strong body without an equally strong mind is worthless. To be a champion you must do more than just work out like one; you must learn to think like one.

Day in and day out strive to perfect your form and your fighting techniques. When you train alone, when you spar, when you are in class, and when you are driving to the tournament, think and act in the same positive manner that you will have when you are on the line at the tournament. However you think and act in practice is how you will think and act at the tournament. In other words, you are what you practice to be.

You might be surprised at the number of competitors who live in a fantasy world where they dream of greatness while living and practicing in mediocrity. These losers keep themselves going with lies like this one: "I just go through the motions when I practice my kicks and punches. On the day of the fight I'll psych myself up." Forget this. It just does not happen this way.

The Power of Self-Talk

Always hold this vision in your mind: first place, first place, first place. Think it and say it and write it and imagine yourself winning first place a zillion times until it becomes as natural for you to see yourself winning first place as breathing water is to fishes. Some disagree with me, but I have always said, "Show me a good loser and I'll show you a loser."

The power of this positive self-talk cannot be overemphasized. Only through self-talk can you overcome the fear of failure that holds 999 out of 1,000 contestants away from the coveted first place position. Only with self-talk can we destroy the evil dream-killing demon known as low self-image.

I believe that low self-image destroys more people than all the sickness in the world combined. So how do we beat low self-image? Can we destroy it with a little pep talk to ourselves before each competition? No way. If you want to beat the scourge of self-doubt, blast yourself with positive self-talk before, during, and after every contest. Twenty-four hours a day this is your jingle: "first place, first place, first place."

Aboe Hada is the World Karate Association (WKA) bantamweight champion of the United States. When I asked him what makes him different from the many contenders he faces in the ring, he responded: "Every time I punch the bag I am screaming to myself, inside my own head, 'I will be champion, I will be champion,' over and over. When I punch the bag, when I spar, all the time I say this to me; that is the difference."

Bill Wallace was a winner and a champion to the core. He found it impossible to perceive himself as anything but a winner. "When I bowed to my opponent and prepared to fight, I always knew that I would win. It never entered my mind that I would lose."

Program yourself to think positive thoughts about all aspects of winning. Allow yourself no negative self-talk. Head off such complaints as "I do not feel well," or "Look how tough the competition is here," or "I already have enough points so this match does not matter." Start your positive self-talk training immediately.

After a few days or weeks of thinking like a winner, you will begin to feel like a winner. You will also begin to notice much loser talk around you. At tournaments you will hear your friends and rivals utter dozens of complaints and reasons why they have a problem and may not do well on this particular day.

These people are setting themselves up to fail. They make a point of explaining their weakness to you so that when they lose you will understand why (the not-my-fault syndrome). In reality they are deciding in advance to lose the contest.

It was shortly after I finally realized that my excuses and negative self-talk were destroying my chances for victory that I began to win consistently. From that point on I went into tournaments mentally prepared to win rather than subconsciously set on losing.

Sometimes the pressures of competition and the stresses of everyday life will combine and make it tough for you to maintain your positive winning mind-set. To get through these times of extreme self-doubt, I employed a technique that I learned from World Champion fighter Joe Lewis.

Tape Talk

Joe Lewis, one of the greatest fighters in the history of American karate, always traveled with a small tape recorder. On occasion I would see him listening to the thing and wonder what he was up to. It was on the day of his championship fight that he finally confided to me the reason for his recorder. Before each bout he played "victory" tapes to himself.

He explained that he filled his victory tapes with positive talk and victory messages. By use of the recorder, Lewis kept his self-image riding high. His tapes reminded him of how hard he had worked, how many hours he had trained, and how much he deserved to win.

Recording positive self-talk is a smart thing to do. When you tape-record all the reasons that you deserve to win and then play the tape back to yourself, you overcome the self-doubts that tend to drown out the positive talk inside your head. These messages are most valuable in the hours and minutes before you compete. These are the moments in which the pressure is greatest, the noise is loudest, and the monster of self-doubt is at his ugly best.

First Place or Bust

When you compete, always have the attitude that you are going to win first place. I do not care if you have the flu. I do not care if you have had a fight with your spouse or whether you just got fired from your job. You owe it to yourself and to your sport to give it your best.

Never shoot for second place. Do not delude yourself. You cannot "win" second place. Second place is a loser's place. No matter who you are up against, never let yourself be happy with second place. Someone who competes simply for the fun of stepping on the line might be thrilled with a second or third place trophy, but you are different. You are a champion, and for you it is first place or bust.

Rising from the Ashes

You are not always going to win first place, at least not for a while. When you fail to get first place you can still turn your loss into a victory of sorts. Instead of getting depressed about what did not happen, study what did happen.

If you walk away with a losing second or third place, or do not place at all, simply ask yourself why. What happened? Did you underperform or were you outperformed? Were you beaten by a superior fighter, or did you beat yourself by failing to take advantage of your opportunities? What were your weak areas? Your strengths? Break it down in your mind, put your analysis on paper, and study the videotape if there is one.

Dwell on your failure. Examine it bit by bit, over and over, until you understand exactly what went wrong. Resolve to correct your mistakes, and get back out there as quickly as possible and compete again, this time without the goofs.

The Fare of Champions

On the day of a tournament I always ate lightly. Like most athletes I could move faster and jump higher with less in my stomach. No food at all, however, was a mistake that I made only one time.

Hungry hounds may run a bit faster, but competing in karate on an empty stomach gives you a solid disadvantage. Starve yourself before a contest and you will be weak and subject to headaches and low energy levels. To be at your best you need food energy; just make sure you eat the right amount and the right kind of food.

Breakfast before a tournament should consist of high-energy foods like fruit and cereal. Eat some bread and drink a protein drink if you like, but make sure not to overeat. Exactly what to eat and how much vary among individuals.

Thurman Karan, Karyn Turner's only student, concentrates on Turner's coaching before the 1989 Internationals Tournament.

If you have a high metabolism, you may be able to eat a heavier breakfast. During the days and weeks before a tournament you should experiment. Make nutrition a part of your training. Keep notes on how your body reacts to different foods.

Sticks and Stones

Until I wised up, I constantly allowed myself to be bullied. I was the steady victim of before-the-fight gamesmanship, verbal battles, and body-language bully tactics.

It is only natural to fear a strong and confident opponent, especially when that opponent is showing off for your benefit. You see him warm up using his best and most favored techniques, and you wonder how you could ever hope to beat him. This is exactly what he wants you to think. Everything that the karate bully says and does before a match is done with the intention of shaking you up.

Never allow yourself to be intimidated by what your competition does before the battle. If you let his actions bully you then, you enter the fight in a greatly weakened psychological condition.

How to Beat the Bully at His Own Game

How can you avoid feeling intimidated by the body language and actions of a karate bully? Just remember that you have put as many hours into your practice as he has, and you can do anything he can. A karate tournament is a game of nerves and skill; it is very much a contest of who can sell himself the best. When an aggressive individual swaggers and brags and warms up with his hottest technique, you can bet he is hungry to win. You can also use his hunger against him.

Studies have shown that a surprisingly large amount of human communication is nonverbal. For example, when a person says "yes" while shaking his head from side to side, the listener will most often assume he means no. I found that the more an opponent tried to use body language to intimidate and bully me, the more she told me about herself. Just by watching her walk about, interact with her pals, and warm up I could figure out her level of self-confidence and much of what she was planning to use in the fight.

Tough Talk

There are two common strategies that fighters use to shake each other up on the day of a competition. Learn now to recognize both methods so that you can avoid their effects. The first strategy is the intimidation approach. The intimidator avoids talking nicely to anyone and is rude to everyone. He is mean and he goes out of his way to glare and to snarl. One of the best in the business was karate great Jim Harrison.

When Harrison walked into an arena everyone shook. He knew people feared him and he played it to the hilt. On many occasions I watched him turn his opponents into jelly simply by giving them his hard look and by barking at them in his frightening way. He always acted the part of the bad guy and most of his opponents acted shell-shocked by his presence.

There was nothing that could be said to him that he did not have a comeback for. He was a master of words. Once I saw a guy walk up to Harrison and say, "You know I am feeling hot today, Harrison."

Harrison did not answer.

The guy said, "You know, it'll take a damn good man to beat me today."

Harrison looked at him and said, "Yeah, but it will not take me long."

Jekyll and Hyde

Harrison talked tough and he fought tough, but after an event he would always show a different personality. When the last fight was over and the day had ended, the real Jim Harrison came out. The truth about this "mean" guy? Do not tell him I said so, but Jim Harrison is one of the nicest guys alive. He was fun to party with and easy to be around. At night Harrison was friendly to everyone, even those he had intimidated so badly during the day.

When the party was over, it was completely over for Harrison and those who dared to compete with him. The next day he would show up at the tournament and take up where he had left off the day before. Immediately he set about his business of striking fear into the hearts of all who came near him. Striding and swaggering, he would march across the arena with glares for everyone and nothing but tough talk on his "cruel" lips. The change was so dramatic I could hardly believe it. He was like a split personality, Dr. Jekyll by night and Mr. Hyde by day.

The Dark Side

Fred Wren, one of my favorite fighters, was another master of intimidation. His ringside behavior was as dark or darker than Harrison's. When Fred Wren walked in, everyone trembled. Without saying a word he had everyone's attention and everyone's respect. His psychological advantage was so great that his opponents were almost always defeated before they got to the ring. When Wren was a defending champion his opponents would frequently fail to show up for the final fight. Those who had the guts to fight him say it was like going up against a creature from one of Stephen King's novels.

The ability to create fear is the great strength of the intimidator. If you can put on a frightening face and if you have a commanding and intimidating bearing, you may be able to use this strategy. If you can make it work, this Dirty Harry ploy creates a strong psychological position from which to fight. All you have to do, if you employ this method, is live with yourself afterwards.

The Good Ole Boy Method

If you are like me you haven't got a mean bone in your body. I doubt that I could sleep at night if I spent my day trying to bully and intimidate other competitors. I was not cut out to be a bad guy. I just did not have the right look. Therefore, before a fight it was necessary for me to adopt other strategies whereby I could gain the upper hand. One such method is particularly effective, if somewhat sneaky. I call it the good ole boy method, and it is the second common strategy to consider.

This deceptive strategy is designed to soften up an opponent by leading him to believe that you are a nice guy (which you are). When you play the good ole boy role you take time to get to know your opponent before you fight him. You make friends, set him at ease, teach him to relax in your presence, and gain his confidence.

By getting your opponent to like you, you will have a strong psychological advantage. The odds are that he will lighten up when he faces you in the ring. He will probably fight you "nice." Unfortunately for him, you will be operating at full bore—blasting away at your new "friend" with merciless accuracy.

Catch Flies with Sugar

Karate champion Howard Jackson loved everybody. He was kind and sweet to everybody before he fought. But when he entered the ring it was as if a curtain had dropped, and he turned into a new person. When he stepped on the line, his eyes seemed to stare right through his opponents. He exploded into them with ferocious and violent energy. He was after blood—it was as if he wanted to kill.

I am certain that Jackson did not use this "relax them and then smash them" strategy on purpose. He is a genuinely warm and wonderful person, and he was so good at what he did that he did not need any prefight strategy. But his nice guy/mean guy way of doing things worked terribly well.

Karate is, as I have said before, an expression of the self. What works for someone else may not work for you. Learn to set up your opponents in a way that suits your personality and stick with it.

Defensive Strategies

You must understand that many of your opponents will be setting you up with strategies of their own. It is important that you continue with your strategy, but it is even more important that you understand why your opponent acts the way he does before a fight. Do not let him sucker you into fighting his fight.

If he tries to talk to you, butter you up, and get you relaxed before the fight, ignore him. Do not let him do it. Find a way to end the conversation and get away from him. Find a place where you can be by yourself and concentrate on your fight.

If your opponent tries to intimidate you verbally, do not react. Ignore him and get away from him. Focus on your fight, and remember that is why you came. You are not there to talk a big game or get bogged down in a psychological battle. You are there to win the tournament.

Prefight mind games did not affect me much because I concentrated on winning, and I kept my distance from other competitors. I did not give others a shot at changing my mood and my level of intensity.

Your rivals are going to use these two strategies with the intention of shaking you up. Now that you understand this, you will not be affected as much as others in your division.

Looking Tough

If you are good and you know that you are good, then your body language will tend to reflect it. When you are confident in your ability to do what you have trained so hard to do, you will radiate an aura of self-assurance that others will notice instantly. This glow of confidence scares the blazes out of your rivals. And if your reputation matches your bearing, your opponents may give up before the fight begins and start bashing it out (in their own heads) for second place—and all this before anyone sets a foot on the competition floor.

It is hard, however, to fool people into thinking you are skilled when you are not. Jim Harrison played the bad guy and Howard Jackson was nice to the extreme, but both of these men were confident in their ability, and everybody could see it in them. Nobody ever questioned their skill level or the level of their authority.

You can strut around with your gut in and your chest out playing the bad guy all day long and still manage to convince very few that you are confident in your ability as a martial artist. Swagger as you may, if you are faking, your subconscious body language will give you away. Your body cannot lie about what your brain knows or does not know. This is why I stress the importance of overtraining, drilling the techniques into yourself until they are nearly perfect.

When your mind and your body are completely trained (and you have a little experience), you will shine with confidence. Everyone will know, without any conscious effort on your part, that you are a force to be reckoned with. Your body will reflect your mental fortitude. Even if you do not look mean you will look strong, confident, and tough.

Butterfly Stomach

At the start of your karate career you will suffer from the shakes until you get some tournament experience under your belt. Even though you overtrain you are going to have to endure some insecurity in the beginning. That is OK; everybody in the lower-ranked divisions must deal with the same anxiety.

In the beginning it may be a question of who trembles least. By reading this book, by attending karate tournaments as a spectator, by training hard, and by talking to veteran competitors, you can reduce your beginner's shakes substantially. As one trainer said, "You will still get butterflies in your stomach but at least you will get them to fly in formation."

Confidence Borrowing

You can also use a technique that I call confidence borrowing to help you through this delicate stage. To understand how confidence bor-

The goal is not only to train your mind and your body completely but to exude confidence.

rowing works, imagine that you are a skilled public speaker. You deliver talks almost daily, and over the years you have stood before countless audiences. You are an expert and you feel little or no fear when you speak. You are completely confident in your ability to hold a crowd with your message and your voice. In contrast, you have no experience as a karate fighter, and though you have been training hard you find yourself shaking like a leaf before your first competition. No one can be confident when he has never done something before, or can he?

Immediately after I had retired from the ring I entered the dog-eat-dog world of professional promoting. My new job required me to go out into corporate America and attempt to secure major sponsors. After years of winning tournaments, I found myself hurtling headlong into a world I knew nothing about.

Suddenly I was charged with negotiating deals involving hundreds of thousands of dollars. I was at a total loss. In this world of numbers and marketing realities that was completely outside of my experience. I could not even speak the language. My self-confidence seemed to dwindle with each appointment—I found myself wishing that I was back in the ring.

The stress and fear came to a head one day when I was in the lobby of the Coors Brewing Company. After three tense meetings with company officials, I had managed to get an appointment with Frank Celeste, an executive at the highest decision-making level. My objective was to get Coors to sponsor a series of televised kickboxing events. As I sat in the outer lobby, I felt that facing off against a big tough opponent with blood in her eyes and murder in her heart would have been child's play compared to the anxiety I was feeling about this meeting.

When my name was called and I walked into the inner reception area, I was trembling like a white belt before her first fight. Thousands of dollars and perhaps the very future of kickboxing was riding on this call, and I knew I had to do something quickly to gain control over my fear. Frantically, I searched my mind for something from the martial arts that would relate to my present situation.

I pretended that instead of facing the major marketing director of the Coors Brewing Company, I was standing up to a karate opponent with a bad reputation. I focused on the image of a big tough woman dressed in a white karate uniform, with a black belt tied around her waist and an evil glint in her eye—it was a familiar image and a challenge that held no fear for me. That is when it happened—confidence from my karate world spilled over into the corporate world. My mind cleared. My anxiety subsided. By the time the secretary told me to go in, the shaking had stopped, my hands were steady, and my heart rate was somewhere near normal.

I entered Celeste's office as an equal. Mentally I borrowed enough confidence from my karate life so that I could hold my head high in this strange new world. Whatever this man was to the marketing industry for beer, I rationalized, I was his equivalent in karate.

I got the sponsorship with Coors and after an eight-year working relationship I am now close friends with Frank Celeste. From time to time we talk about that important meeting we had in his office so long ago. He always comments on how confident I was that day—little does he know.

Control Your Fear

Confidence borrowing provided the breakthrough that I needed to do well in that meeting with Celeste and to establish myself as a player in this new game. With confidence borrowing I was able to control my fear and to minimize that feeling of helplessness that always strikes us when we try something new. I have used this technique many times since, and I have discovered that it is a common tool used by people from all walks of life, including politicians, public speakers, and professional athletes. Confidence borrowing is a winner's trick. When you are about to enter your first competition, you will find confidence borrowing an especially helpful tool.

No doubt you are an expert at one or more things. Perhaps you are a lawyer, confident in the face of a judge and jury; or maybe you are a painter, confident as you stand at the top of your ladder. Whatever it is that you do well, mentally borrow confidence from it when you face your first karate opponent. Just imagine he is a building in need of sanding and paint or a legal opponent in need of a verbal pounding. If you are a beginner, try it immediately. Your borrowed confidence will blow the other rookies away. They may wonder what you are doing in their division.

Winning the Head Game

I have only one student now, Thurman Karan. Thurman was very young when he began his karate training, and he was only eight when he and I flew to California for his first try at the Internationals Tournament. Already he was a proven fighter and a consistent winner in his age and rank division.

The Internationals is such a huge event that it scares even the bravest of people. I warned Thurman to expect some mind games from his competition, and I gave him tips on how to deal with them. Although confident and experienced, Thurman was small and shy by nature. In those stressful moments before the fighting began, he looked more than a little frightened. It was not long before one of his bolder rivals singled him out as an easy mark for verbal and nonverbal harassment.

As Thurman stood shoulder to shoulder with the boys in his division, a larger boy beside him said, "I am going to smash your face, punk" (or something very close to that). From the sidelines I saw Thurman's eyes roll and his forehead knot. I could tell that he was

Thurman Karan, his training and confidence paying off, holds a pose among some of his trophies.

struggling to maintain his composure and to ignore the bigger boy's comments.

When the larger boy shoved him, Thurman's face turned scarlet. He held his body rigid, an expression of fear etched across his face. He glanced over at me, his blue eyes pleading for guidance. Deliberately, I ignored his nonverbal request for help. I watched to see if he could handle the situation on his own.

When the bully shoved Thurman a second time and Thurman did nothing, I began to worry. As I walked closer, the big kid pushed him a third time, nearly knocking Thurman off his feet. Before I could say anything the bully lifted his arms to push poor Thurman a fourth time. But suddenly, to my delight, Thurman reached out and grabbed the big kid's arm before he could initiate the fourth push. Holding the other's arm, Thurman looked his antagonist hard in the eyes and said, "Not again." His voice and his eyes had all the power of Dirty Harry's "Go ahead, make my day." The bully jerked his arm back, eyes wide. The aggressive kid turned his attention to some easier target.

Smiling, I returned to my seat. Thurman had won an important head game. More important, he had gained a new level of confidence that would serve him well in countless events to come. By the way, Thurman won the championship in fighting in his division at the Internationals that year.

Lining Up the Right Way

When it is your time to fight, the referee calls your name and the name of your opponent. At this point you and your rival will advance to the line and face off. How you get to the line and which side of the line you stand on are both important.

It is a fact that 99 out of 100 competitors saunter to the line. Perhaps it is human nature to go slowly into battle. There is something about combat, even the controlled sort of fighting that point karate is supposed to be, that we all fear. You cannot get rid of all your own fear, but you can add greatly to your opponent's fear if you rush forward to meet him.

Rush to Fight!

Always run to the line. Get there first no matter what. The psychological impact of running to the fighting line will provide you with an overwhelming advantage over your slow-moving opponent. In addition, the referee, the judges, and the audience see you charge forward, eager and seemingly unafraid. At the same time they see your opponent walking slowly, perhaps reluctantly, out to meet you.

I found running to the line to be such an effective power move that I did it at every event. I even took it a step further by going to the scorekeeper and finding out exactly when I was to compete. Rather than wait for my name to be called and then rush to the line I would rush to the line before they called my name. I enjoyed the emotional advantage of being first, and running to the line also allowed me to pick which side of the line I would fight from.

Pick the Side with a "View"

In point karate, one side of the fighting line is almost always better than the other. By watching the referee and considering the position of the judges, I would determine which side would best show off my techniques. Then I would rush out to get it.

One side is better than the other because the referee, not the judges, makes most of the point calls. Most referees tend to work the fights from one side and in one general area. Always pick the side that you believe will give your referee the best view of your punches and kicks.

The Power Stare

Once at the line and facing your opponent, stare directly into his eyes. It may be difficult for you, painful almost, to maintain eye contact with your rival at such a tense moment, but you must force yourself to do it. When you look directly and steadily into your opponent's eyes, you tell him that you are unafraid. The message is that you are confident and that you are ready to fight. The psychological impact of your stare is tremendous.

It was difficult for me to stare into my opponent's eyes as we faced off across the line. I tried it several times and with each attempt I suffered from great anxiety. Finally I learned to look directly at the person's forehead. For some reason this made it very easy for me to maintain constant "eye" contact. And my opponents, as far as I know, never knew that my eyes were gazing at their hairline rather than into the whites of their eyes.

When you face off with your opponent, stare directly into his eyes.

Before You Do Your Kata

As you stand ready to perform your kata you must radiate confidence. Hold your head high, stand with good posture, and just before you begin give the judges a smile.

Forms competition is much different from fighting, and though you are about to do a serious form, you should show the judges that you like performing and that you are happy to be there doing what you do. Most judges are karate black belts and avid martial arts practitioners and competitors. Most appreciate the fact that you seem to enjoy doing what you are doing.

Do not fire a big snail-eating grin at them. A pleasant, happy expression will do nicely. It may seem like a simple secret but it is no small thing. That little smile produces a magic feeling in the judges' hearts.

Wear your serious face as you do your form, and let your half smile return when you complete the set. Unlike karate fighting, kata competition is not combat; it is meant to be fun to watch, thrilling perhaps, but not life and death. If you look like you are having a good time, then spectators and the judges will enjoy watching you.

Wake-Up Calls for Judges

Wake-up calls, special preform actions, are now commonplace at the major karate events. My regular method of waking up the judges was to enter the ring, execute a triple butterfly kick, then stomp on the floor. I did it to let those judges and everyone else in the arena know that I was coming. After startling everyone, I would bow and walk to the center of the ring to perform my kata.

In weapons competition I would sometimes use wake-up movements that had little to do with martial arts. When competing with the Chinese sword, I would run to the ring and toss my blade into the air. I threw it with a spin so that it traveled high and came hurtling down in what appeared to be a dangerous spiral. To the amazement of the crowd I would catch the weapon by the handle and then continue my dash into the ring. This blew the crowd away and made the judges sit up straight.

This sword-tossing technique is very simple to do and not dangerous in the least. Just be sure you throw the weapon straight up so that it will fall straight back down. It should spiral with the hilt below the blade. Do not pitch it into a horizontal spin or you will lose control and look like a fool.

Action mixed with sound makes for a great wake-up combination. The moment that my student Thurman Karan's name is called he hits the floor with both sticks, quickly clacks the sticks together, and spins around and hits them again. It is a flashy movement combined with the loud whack, whack, whack of the sticks as they hit. He walks to the center of the ring, and for effect he does it again—whack, whack, whack—and everyone is awake.

You can wake up your judges and gain notoriety for yourself if you perform a flashy movement that is uniquely your own. Do it often and it becomes your trademark, a symbol of your skill and the signature of your performance. One day you might even notice someone else using your trademark wake-up call to enhance their own odds of winning. Recently, at the Battle of Atlanta tournament, I was flattered to see a

Wake the judges up with a flashy preform maneuver. Turner, seen here with a Chinese broad sword, frequently tossed her sword high into the air and caught it by its handle.

young woman wake up her audience and her judges by performing a spinning body wrap that began high and continued until she had spun all the way to the floor. This was an exact duplicate of a wake-up movement designed for me years ago by my instructor, Al Dacascos.

Trademark movements are not difficult to come up with. Let your creative mind flow; you will be surprised at your ability to devise stylish preform movements.

Your Opening Speech

Your introductory speech can be an eye-opener. Avoid monotones and flat rhythms when you talk. Tell the judges who you are in a voice that demands attention. Add a little theater to your introduction—mix up your voice patterns by matching high and low tones. Done right, your voice can demand the attention of the sleepiest judge.

Opening with Comedy

In certain divisions you can wake up the judges with a bit of comedy. I saw a good example of this recently when two young men did a real number on the judges and everyone in the arena. It was a specialty forms division that allowed two-man forms and other special martial arrangements.

They introduced themselves and began their form. After a technique or two a heckler from the audience started shouting. He physically disrupted the form while claiming the two were frauds and that their performance was a sham and an insult to traditional karate. The competitors stopped their set and dealt with the intruder physically before hundreds of startled fans.

The joke was on us—the heckler was a plant. By inserting a bit of drama these guys fired up the judges and entertained their audience. While their martial technique was no better than, and perhaps inferior to, many of the other contestants, their showmanship was first class and they walked off with the first place trophy.

Open divisions and specialty divisions offer many such opportunities to wake up the judges and gain the support of the crowd. But make sure you use comedy in good taste. Do it only in special divisions that allow such goings-on. Misplaced comedy will not be funny to anyone except perhaps your competition.

Adapt, Conform, and Overcome

At one tournament you may find judges from a variety of styles. At the next event you could get a majority of soft stylists. At still another contest you may be faced with a panel made up exclusively of hard stylists, as happened to me many times during my career.

You will face many such biased judges. If you find your blood pressure rising in the face of this unfairness, just remember that these guys are not out to punish you. They simply have no criteria to make their judgments from other than the criteria of their own system. This is the reality of the point circuit. If you fight it you will end your karate career in frustration.

Aim Only for First Place

The process of winning begins long before you enter the ring. You train your body for victory and program your mind for success. The contest for first place begins the second you set foot inside the arena and lasts throughout the day and beyond. Every word you speak and every move you make has an effect on the outcome and must be intended to help you win first place.

Victory in forms and fighting depends on your actions and your ability to get reactions from your opponent. You must also be able to determine which of the four types of opponent you are up against, the subject of Chapter 3.

3
The Four Types
of Fighters

In boxing there are "sluggers" and there are "boxers." Mike Tyson is a slugger; Mohammed Ali was a boxer. Tyson will slam your head right off your shoulders and leave you in a near-dead heap on the floor. Ali would poke you in the face and body with quick, stinging combinations. He would hit you time after painful time until he had slaughtered you on points.

Most boxers fit into one description or the other. Is it surprising to learn that there are only four types of karate fighters? For a long time I could not accept this truth. I felt that each opponent was an entirely new entity, and I fought every fight as if it were my first.

Tournament Terror

My frustration began early in my first months as a student of the Korean martial art known as tae kwon do. After competing in several closed tae kwon do tournaments, I realized that I was not a natural fighter. My instructors taught me techniques and gave me good advice, but I could not make them work. When I won I was at a loss to say why. When I lost I was just as unsure as to the cause.

When I made the switch from tae kwon do to the softer, more fluid, Chinese system taught by Al Dacascos, I was in a state of utter frustration. Dacascos, a veteran competitor in the open circuits, quickly informed me that it was not my style that was lacking. He believed that there were no superior styles, only superior fighters. With Al's help I was soon fighting in open karate tournaments.

With each fight I faced a new opponent and a totally new problem in strategy. In spite of what Al tried to teach me, it seemed that there was no pattern to karate combat. The confusion and frustration I had felt in my tae kwon do tournament days returned with a fury.

I lived my karate life in fear. Since I was at the bottom of my weight class, virtually all of my opponents were larger than I was. There were only two weight divisions for women and at 126 pounds I fell into the heavier. My strategy, if you could call it that, was to get my points before they could smash me.

All during this period of terror Al was hard at work trying to teach

Karyn Turner demonstrates a posture from the Chinese martial arts system taught by Al Dacascos, her instructor (here and on next page).

 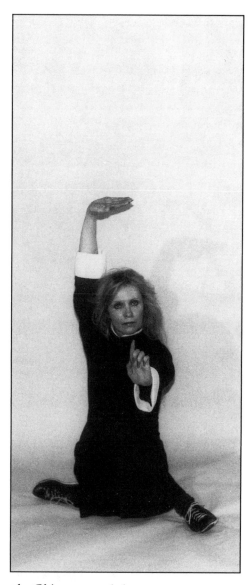

Turner demonstrates more postures from the Chinese martial arts system.

me the 18 Principles of Winning. When the concepts finally sank in, it was as if I had been born again. I began to see the patterns and the connections that make karate work. Overnight my fears disappeared. Suddenly I liked to fight and I preferred fighting bigger women!

Bigger women were slower and therefore easier to defeat with the concepts from the 18 Principles. And best of all I understood at last what Al had been trying to get me to see: in all the world there are only four types of fighters.

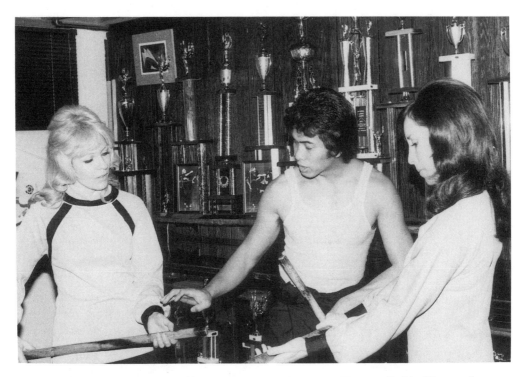

Al Dacascos discusses tournament tactics with Karyn Turner (left). He taught that there were no superior styles, only superior fighters.

The Four Types of Fighters

Both Joe Lewis and Al Dacascos learned of Bruce Lee's fighting principles through direct association with him. Linda Lee, Bruce's widow, later imparted even more complete information regarding these all-important concepts. If not for Al Dacascos and Bruce and Linda Lee, I would have been out there fighting a thousand different types of opponents. Or worse I would have quit early and never gone on to enjoy my years as a karate champion.

My karate life was changed forever by these principles. Winning ceased to be a matter of luck and became instead a matter of skill. It would be a while before I earned the distinction of being a champion, but it was at the moment when I realized there were only four opponents out there and that I had the principles needed to beat all four that I became—in my heart—a true champion.

I quickly developed strategies that would beat the four opponents. It became unnecessary for me to use a wide variety of techniques; I dropped the fancy stuff and concentrated on the basics. The straight punch, reverse punch, sidekick, roundkick, and the backfist became my arsenal. When I started winning every tournament in sight, magazine and sports writers started looking me up for interviews and photographs. In short order, Karyn Turner became a recognized name in the sport of karate.

Privately, however, those who knew me before my breakthrough admitted that they could not see a difference in what I was doing in the ring. No one outside of a close circle of friends and classmates understood why I was suddenly winning.

At this same time Joe Lewis was also winning tournaments and fame for himself by using the principles. Lewis got lots of criticism because he used a very limited number of techniques. As it was with me, no one could quite understand why he always won.

The Same Four Fighters Are Out There Today!

As a martial arts coach and promoter I attend several major tournaments each year. Believe me, things have changed very little in the tournament world in the years since my retirement from competition. If anything the quality and caliber of competition has declined slightly in the last few years.

Since karate as a sport has not gotten particularly tougher in these few years, where are the nineties versions of Bill Wallace and Joe Lewis? Why aren't there more superstars?

Perhaps it is because so few fighters know and apply the winning principles. And how many competitors realize that only four types of fighters make up the karate universe? How many veteran fighters are out there guessing about strategy, unable to determine exactly what type of opponent they are up against?

There are still good trainers out there to be sure. But most of their champions win titles by virtue of their natural athletic abilities. Today's competitors are gamblers who at best win more than 50 percent of the time, never knowing why they win or lose.

Not everyone wants to hear that there is a pattern or method to karate greatness. Some students ignore the wisdom of the principles and the four types of fighter concept. They go on fighting their own way against endless dozens of types of opponents. I saw this firsthand years ago when I tried to help a friend and fellow student who had difficulty grasping the idea that there were only four types of fighter.

In fact she had difficulty learning, or perhaps in accepting, any of the 18 Principles.

My efforts to help her grasp the principles ended in frustration and disappointment. Consequently she was never able to win consistently. She was an excellent technician, but her grasp of fighting was never firm. When she came against an opponent who made any sort of change, such as altering the timing a bit or switching lead sides from right to left, she would lose the fight.

Some people find it difficult to accept the fact that there is more to karate than technique. You will find plenty of fighters on the sidelines who will argue that Bruce Lee's concept of four fighter types is a simplistic farce. Some break down the various styles of fighters into five groups or maybe into six or even sixty. Let these critics have it their own way. When they see you winning match after match perhaps they will reevaluate the wisdom of Lee's principles.

Winning Thoughts

Tournament fighting is a thinking person's game. Unlike a street fight where anything goes, a karate tournament provides a highly controlled environment for the test of combat skills.

The limitations of the format make it especially easy to determine which type of fighter you are pitted against. The controlled environment makes it easier, not harder, to use all of the 18 Principles of Winning.

The limitations make it possible for you to win quickly and easily against any opponent no matter how large or how powerful. Even if he is better than you are in all of his techniques, you can beat him every time because you know exactly what type of fighter he is. You know where he is coming from, how he is coming, and why. With the principles you have him. Whether he is a charger, a blocker, a runner, or an elusive runner, he is yours.

Determining which one of the four types of opponents you are facing is a matter of great importance. Often you can get his number by simply watching him fight in a match before your own. If you do not get that opportunity you will have to test him inside the ring. The faster you find out which of the four types you are up against, the faster you can defeat him.

The Charger

The charger, also called the jammer, is the one who attempts to run over you. He is the most assertive of all fighters. He rushes at you with full force again and again, forcing you to fight or to flee. He proceeds to chase you and blast away until he gets you or until you get him.

The charger is an aggressive off-the-line fighter, and his strategy is very sound. The main strength of his style is his ability to spring off the line and score a point before his opponent can respond. A great example of a charger can be seen in Bruce Lee's movie *Enter the Dragon*. Bruce faces an evil opponent at a tournament of karate masters. Three times, as the referee signals, Lee springs forward and strikes the man in the face before the poor guy is able to react.

In real life Howard Jackson is without a doubt the best first-strike charger that I have ever seen. He did his initial moves better than the fastest fighters of his time. Jackson was particularly effective as a charger because he was quick and because he stayed low to the ground

Howard Jackson (right) charges into his opponent.

when he attacked. He always kept his body level and on balance as he thundered forward and penetrated his opponent's critical-distance line. His attack was over and the point earned before his opponent knew what hit him. His attacks happened in one incredible split second of fury and forward motion.

Jackson had the ability to push off with his back leg with such a blur of force that there were times when the only thing you saw of his attack was his opponent's body moving backward. Jackson's whole body moved as a power unit, almost quicker than the eye could register. He remained completely relaxed as he exploded in short fast steps. Even the legendary Fred Wren got his teeth filled with fist at least once when he matched his own formidable and aggressive style against the lightning initial moves of Howard Jackson.

The first time Wren and Jackson clashed, Wren defeated Jackson in a sudden death. "Fighting Fred Wren was like fighting a rhinoceros," Jackson said.

But by the time they met again in 1973 at the Battle of Atlanta, Jackson had gained considerable experience. Like everyone else I was curious to see what would happen. I was also hoping to learn something from the exchange. I had watched Wren fight many times, but I knew Howard Jackson by reputation only. The pitched battle that followed was no disappointment.

My instructor Al Dacascos and I managed to find seats that gave us a good view of Wren and Jackson as they faced off at the line. We watched closely, but when the referee said go the only thing I saw was Fred Wren's head lurching backward. Shocked, I turned to Al and exclaimed, "Did you see that?"

Al shook his head. His eyebrows rose and his jaw dropped. "Yeah," he said finally. "And I want to see it again."

To our amazement Jackson rocked Wren a second time. This time Jackson faked high and struck low, hitting Wren with a reverse punch.

Howard Jackson remembers it this way: "I got two points and then I hit him again, but the referee didn't call it. Fred grabbed me and swept me down and punched me. I decided to go after him with combinations until they pulled me off."

As I recall, this fierce battle ended with Jackson ahead 3–2. Jackson beat the odds that day by shaking Wren's timing.

Jackson used his super charger fighting style to win against other great fighters of his day, including Bill Wallace and Jeff Smith. In 1973 at the U.S. Championships in Dallas Jackson fought eight or

Turner charges her training partner, Kenny Street.

nine fights in one day, winning all but one of them by a spread of 3-zip. One fight he won 3-2. Without question Jackson was the master of the charge.

In 1973 Howard Jackson fought Jeff Smith. According to Jackson, Smith was the toughest opponent he fought. By tough he meant physically tough. Smith used lots of combinations and in general fought with a charging strategy.

When Smith and Jackson clashed at the Battle of Atlanta, they charged at each other repeatedly. In some exchanges Smith started first, forcing Jackson backward and overpowering him. So Jackson turned up his speed and forced Smith to move backward. When Smith hesitated Jackson exploded forward again and followed him in with combinations. He won against Smith that day by mixing the principles of initial speed with broken rhythm.

How to Spot a Charger

There are lots of fighters who use the charging style, and you will be able to spot them very quickly. In fact, the charger is probably the easiest of the four types of fighters to identify.

Chargers are the ones who rush forward from the line. They keep charging primarily in straight-line attacks. They rarely back up or run away.

What to Do Against a Charger

Because he is aggressive, the charger has a powerful psychological advantage. He has also got body weight, momentum, and the strength of forward motion on his side. Armed with the 18 Principles of Winning, however, you can find the chinks in the charger's armor.

Although the charger is tough and aggressive, he is actually the easiest type of fighter against whom to apply the principles. The first rule for dealing with him is to do your counterattack without backing straight up. Backing straight away from a charger is death because he is coming in at full tilt and you are backing out in a hasty stumble. Even if you manage to exchange blows with him, his techniques will appear stronger because he has forward motion and is acting in the aggressive mode.

The charger always tries to make the first move. In doing so he gives you a moment to counter. Since you know he is going to move first, you have an extra half second to decide upon a workable counter.

Principle 17, Angles of Attack, works well against the charger. In this case the direct angle is usually best. By incorporating direct angle of attack with Principle 4, Initial Speed (your first move of an exchange), you can beat the charger at his own game. The moment he starts to move—any part of his body—you must push off directly into him. It takes guts to do this because it is almost a head-on collision, but it is the most effective way to thwart a charger.

You can sidestep a charger, but do not step directly to the side. A side step is too noticeable. It is too easy for your opponent to follow you if you evade him at this angle. To gain the advantage, move at a 45-degree angle. You will be safer, and you will be able to reach him even if he stops his forward motion.

If you are not fast enough to catch the charger on his way in, you can gain time and position by taking a half step to the rear and then pushing yourself forward across his critical-distance line and into the thick of his movement. Your strategy is to fade back slightly, and then go for him with a strong straight punch or kick. This method gives you a little more time, but you still need to be fast.

Timing is everything when dealing with a charger. If, for example, he attacks you with a kick, you have to time your counter to arrive at the precise moment his kicking leg returns to the ground. It is at this point, and only at this point, that his balance will be off.

Kicks work well against a charger. When you are being charged you are automatically on the defensive and therefore at a disadvantage from the viewpoint of the referee and the judges. If you keep enough distance between yourself and the charger to allow yourself to land a kick, you demonstrate to the point callers that you have complete control and superior position.

Principle 18, Broken Rhythm, gives you the ability to sucker the charger into your trap. Let him push you backward for the first couple of exchanges, and then when he comes in again, take a half step back and use your sidekick, your reverse punch, or another devastating technique.

Secrets of the Charger

Great chargers explode into their opponents. They are masters of the initial move. The charger uses his back leg to push off with a thunderous forward rush. He hits his target and never loses his balance. The successful charger never forgets that the shortest distance between two lines is the direct angle of attack, a straight line.

Speed is crucial to effective charging. Surprisingly, many fighters think speed comes from tension. The reverse is true. To get speed into your charge you must stay as relaxed as possible, and then explode into your movement with contracting muscle power.

Howard Jackson stays completely relaxed until he begins his charge. By staying relaxed you too can have maximum mobility and command maximum speed from yourself. Your opponent is unable to read any intention from your relaxed body. Like Jackson, push off hard with your back foot, and then compress all your power into your initial move.

Keep your head level when you charge. If you put your head forward too much you will be off balance and headed for trouble, probably in the form of a fist in your face. Boxers and karate fighters joke about this off-balance charge. They call it "leading with your head." Stay on

Turner practices the "charging step" that she learned from Howard Jackson.

balance as you charge forward. To get the points, you must keep your head above your body's center and your knees bent.

When Howard Jackson sustained an injury at a tournament and was out of competition for a few weeks, he agreed to help me learn his secrets of the initial move. Jackson's teaching was a major boost to my career as a martial artist and my tenure as a champion. Now that it's all in the past, I can finally admit how much I hated the training!

At the dojo (training hall), Jackson pushed me to the limits of endurance day after day, making me sprint up and down the floor with my knees bent and my head level. That was the extent of the training! All day long I was pushing off with my back foot and running forward, always pushing for speed and striving to stay balanced.

Jackson's secret was no secret! He simply made me push and run a million times until it became second nature. I must have looked like some weird animal to the other students—push and run, push and run, hour after miserable hour until my legs screamed and my knees ached.

Through this simple method and under Jackson's expert eye, I managed to add explosive power and much greater speed to my initial moves. Earlier I had been lunging forward; now I was charging in, blasting away with fast, powerful first-strike moves.

The Blocker

Most fighters are blockers—perhaps as many as 80 percent of them. The blocker is identified by his stand-and-counter fighting style. He stays in position and waits for you to make a move. Then he blocks and counters when you come in.

The blocker's strength lies in the fact that he uses very few move-

Turner faces Street and prepares to attack (see next page).

Turner attacks Street and prepares to block (see next page).

ments to accomplish his strategy. He does not need to worry about offense because he rarely attacks. His method is based on simplicity, and his strategy is totally dependent on what you try to do to him.

A good blocker has quick reflexes and a very strong fighting stance. His most common counterattacking technique is the reverse punch. He is always well planted when he fires off his retaliation strike, so he is able to put a great deal of power into the blow. Do not underestimate this style of fighting. The blocker can hurt you because he stands his ground and fights from a position of strength.

The blocker will try to hit you after you throw your first technique and before you can fire off your second. He is a between-the-beats fighter. If, for example, you throw a frontkick at him he will wait until your foot touches the ground and then try to punch you.

Turner stays in position and blocks. About 80 percent of all karate competitors are blockers by definition.

How to Spot a Blocker

If you watch your opponent fight you can quickly determine whether or not he is a blocker. If you do not get the chance to watch him in advance, you can use a fake or two to flush out his style. Stamp your foot hard on the matt and throw your hip out a little as if you are about to kick. If he steps back and plants, you have got a blocker. If he runs away, he is something else. Keep faking until you are sure what you are up against.

What to Do Against a Blocker

A blocker hates to move; therefore you must make him move. He likes to take a half step backward, sink into his solid defensive stance, and pound you with powerful counterstrike techniques. Your job is to shake him out of his rooted position. You do it by assaulting him from unusual and unexpected angles. Odd angles force him to step out of his rigid defensive stance and give you the opening you need to score your points.

When you come in on his blind side, for example, you force him to turn to face you. You make him take up the chase. He has no choice but to follow you because he cannot just stand there with his back to you.

From his blind side you can deliver a solid blow. He, on the other hand, cannot hit you with his reverse punch or his back leg because he is all crossed up. You can kick him or reach over the top of his lead hand and clobber him with a backfist or straight jab.

Do not worry that he might pick up his lead leg and hit you with a sidekick. He cannot do it. In order to gain positioning to hit you with his powerful back leg, he must first pick up his front leg, not to kick but rather to follow your motion. That is your window of opportunity—the moment you should strike. He is most vulnerable at the moment when he steps out of his solid defensive stance.

Fakes work very well on blockers. Hip, body, and shoulder fakes all make him commit himself and throw off his timing.

Throw your fakes with power; make it look like you are coming at him with fully committed techniques. Then change the angle of your attack and force him to react. Design your fakes to force the blocker to move in ways that are uncomfortable for him.

Imply power in your fakes but do not overextend your limbs. If you do you will not be able to recover fast enough to throw your real attack before he regains his solid defensive position.

The blocker's footwork is not outstanding. He is at a disadvantage anytime he is forced to move around. The blocker is at the mercy of the "principled" fighter who assaults him with Principle 17, Angles of Attack.

Principle 18, Broken Rhythm, works well on a blocker, too. Attack and defense patterns, which mix active and passive behaviors in an unpredictable pattern, will disorient a blocker and make him take a step. The blocker relies on timing. He must time his counters and attacks perfectly in order to score. By changing your rhythm and timing you destroy his timing and therefore his strategy.

I won many fights against opponents who used the blocking strategy. First I would move in and throw combinations of techniques that ran right to the edge of the critical-distance line. Each time I would stop, however, before penetrating the line. I took care to launch my attacks at the same speed and with the same timing.

After a few false charges, I would come in for real—this time with a completely new rhythm. With few exceptions the blocker was unable to adapt to the new timing, and I gained my point with ease.

Blockers are analytical fighters. If your broken rhythms work and you get in there and hit him in the head, he will expect you to do it again. So then you fake high and hit him low—it works every time.

The Backward Runner

I hate a backward runner. Every time you move toward him he backs up. He will back up all night long if you let him. The backward runner is an unpleasant type of opponent to face though not a particularly hard type to beat.

Turner demonstrates the backward-runner retreat—backing away in a straight line from an opponent. This strategy is the easiest to beat.

Backing away from an opponent in a straight line is a weak defense. Many backward runners lose points and subsequently the match by constantly backing over the line.

The weaknesses of this strategy are many. It is virtually impossible to maintain balance while running backward. The backward-runner seldom earns a point because his technique is thrown from a submissive position. He is hardly at an advantage as he runs for his life in the face of an aggressive attacker.

The backward-runner strategy has only one strength. Sometimes he runs so hard that he throws his opponent's timing off. This is a weak advantage at best, and I am certain that there has never been a successful fighter who relied on this strategy.

How do you spot a backward runner? Just say "boo" and he will run. Throw any sort of fake and the backward runner backs up. Unlike the blocker who falls back into a solid stance, the backward runner always runs backward in a straight line.

What to Do Against a Backward Runner

Do not waste your time and energy trying to run down a backward runner. Do not use hard fakes or he will just take off. Take your time; creep closer and closer toward his critical-distance line. Make him think that he is safer than he really is. Then when you have him eating out of your hand, salt his tail with a punishing series of high-speed strikes.

Chase him with combinations at a slow pace. Use simple combinations such as a step-kick/step-kick sequence to make him think he knows your range. Then speed up and penetrate by applying hyperextension or double hyperextension (Principle 11, Reach) to knock him loose.

You can also catch the backward runner by chasing him, as long as you chase him at a slow speed. Act nervous and hyperactive as you close in, but do not turn up your speed or really try to get him. Each time saunter back to the line with movements that belie your true speed. Suddenly, push off hard and fast and hit him before he runs. Now you can take him out like Grant took Richmond because his brain is locked into the false speed that you established to fool him.

A third strategy for smashing a backward runner is to wait him out. Someone has to do something sooner or later. By doing nothing at all you will make him so nervous he will change his style and come to you. Then stick him.

Turner's opponent evades her attack by using the elusive-runner strategy. The elusive runner is the most frustrating type of opponent.

The Elusive Runner

The elusive runner is easily the most frustrating type of opponent. Every time you move at him he runs away, but you never know which way he will run. Sometimes he backs up; sometimes he runs right or left. It is an unpredictable and therefore challenging strategy to overcome.

As a point fighter Bill Wallace is best classified as an elusive runner. He used the winning principles to get inside his opponent's defenses, strike with rapid fury, and then get away. His left leg was so deceptive and so quick that few could get away from its sting. He got his point and then ran, avoiding all but the very fastest of counterstrikes. "I was sneaky," Wallace said. "I would get you to chase me and get you to run into something."

Wallace says he ran because he did not like to get hit. Who does? "Pain hurts," the superstar said. "It ruins your whole day. I never wanted to get hit."

Don Wilson is another champion fighter who used an elusive-runner strategy to earn his stripes. For years Wilson held the title of light heavyweight in full contact karate.

"Wilson is much like me," Wallace observed. "Elusive. He moved in and out on you."

The elusive runner is less common than the backward runner. He is still, however, a runner. And running away is sometimes perceived as weak by judges, referees, and fans. It takes a strong fighter like Wallace or Wilson to get the most out of an elusive-runner strategy.

As Bill Wallace proved, an elusive runner is considerably harder to outmaneuver than the backward runner. If you run after him you take the chance of losing your balance or falling into his trap. If you do not chase him the fans will boo and the judges may penalize you for boring them. What can you do?

What to Do Against an Elusive Runner

You can defeat an elusive runner with footwork. Deceptive footwork will enable you to beat him to the draw and turn his strategy against him. Use active and passive patterns of motion mixed with attacks on the direct angle to get the elusive runner to run right into your waiting arms and feet.

By creeping, switch stepping, and triangle stepping, you work your way into his strike zone. Once in range, cut him off by moving to his back side. When he turns around and starts to run, you are already in his critical-distance line, and wham! You got him.

I loved to hit elusive runners with my lead hand. By striking with my lead I caught them off guard. I bridged the gap quickly before they could run by striking without telegraphing my intent.

You can use faking against an elusive runner, but you must fake him along a direct angle. Fake in straight lines because you want him to commit himself. The elusive runner is, well, elusive. He will not respond as you wish unless your fake is extremely realistic. Make your fakes inside his critical-distance line to get the best reactions.

Wallace's running style served him well, and he lost very few fights in his outstanding career. Even Howard Jackson was not fast enough to catch Wallace. When Jackson won against Wallace he did so by immobilizing Wallace's leg. More than once he faked a sweep, leg-checked Wallace's kicking leg, and then pushed off with his back foot and struck before Wallace could run.

Battle Plans

Create a battle plan to be used against each of the four types of fighters. At every opportunity make notes both mental and on paper regarding the things that work or do not work against each type. Gradually you will develop a plan that will quickly knock the steam out of the charger, the blocker, the backward runner, and the elusive runner.

A Fifth Type of Fighter?

When the breakthrough came and I realized that there were only four types of fighters, I felt like a fool. Could it really be that easy? Chargers, blockers, backward runners, and elusive runners—is that all there is to it?

After fighting, coaching, and witnessing hundreds of matches I am still convinced that there are only four main types of fighters in the karate world. As simple as it sounds, if you can beat these four fighters you can beat almost anybody in the world. Ninety-seven percent of all competitors use one of the four styles of fighting almost exclusively.

Which fighting style should you adapt? Which will work best for you? The answer? All four—you must become all four types of fighters. By adapting the 18 Principles of Winning to each of the four styles you will become not one type of fighter but many types in the eyes of your opponents. In all of the karate world only about three percent, the best of the best, use a combination of all four styles to defeat their opponents. Welcome to an elite group!

4
The Five Primary
Techniques

In his principles of winning Bruce Lee identified five primary techniques: the backfist, the reverse punch, the sidekick, the roundkick, and the backkick. Why only five? It was certainly not because he was afraid of variety; after all, he investigated and borrowed techniques and concepts from twenty-seven different martial arts systems when he devised his personal fighting style *Jun Fan*, also known as *jeet kuen do* (JKD). But it says a lot that after such an exhaustive study of so many different styles that Lee identified the above five techniques as the most basic and most effective of all—the primary techniques.

Karate practitioners love new techniques. In tournament competition, however, it is not the number of techniques you possess that count; it is the ability to use the techniques in concert with the 18 Principles of Winning. By so doing you can amplify the possibilities of one technique into thousands of different applications.

Let us begin with the first of the five primary techniques, the backfist. First I will describe the technique, and then I will explain how you can use the principles to multiply the opportunities.

Turner chambers her arm and prepares to deliver a traditional backfist (see next page).

The Backfist

The referee said go and I charged forward from the line; then I lifted my knee as if to throw a sidekick. My opponent was taller, as usual, and outweighed me a bit. I knew she was a quick fighter so I came in at full speed. She dropped her right to cover her ribs in anticipation of my kick. That is when I released the real technique, a backfist. Pow— it landed right on her jaw. The point was mine.

We faced off again. I lunged at her and threw my lightning backfist at her face. She brought her hands high in an effort to avoid getting backfisted a second time. This time the backfist was only a fake. I used it to cover the real technique—a skipping sidekick. I got the point and so did she, I think.

There are two main types of backfist—the traditional one and the

Turner delivers a traditional backfist which is not usually used in sport karate. The chambering motion takes too much time and telegraphs your intention.

modern tournament one. A tournament-style backfist is your fastest weapon. It is also the closest weapon to your opponent's face and therefore represents his greatest fear.

The traditional karate backfist is stilted and does not work well in open tournaments. To perform it you must fold your arm into your body and then swing it out. The attack angle is approximately 35 degrees. The chambering motion takes too much time and telegraphs your intention. You can see a traditional backfist coming from two miles away.

The modern karate backfist by contrast is very fast and gives your opponent absolutely no warning. Mechanically speaking the modern backfist is almost the same movement as a boxer's jab.

Karyn Turner demonstrates the modern, tournament-style backfist (see next page).

Like the jab the modern backfist begins from a point just in front of your face. It does not chamber back to the body, and it does not swing out in a wide arc. It is a quick, sleek attack that fires along a line that is very nearly straight. The main difference is in the strike zone. The backfist hits with the back of the hand while the boxer's jab strikes with the knuckles.

Boxers push off into their jab to enhance the power. But they don't try to cover much distance. Karate fighters use their backfist to cover distance. Because they are looking to close a wider gap, karate fighters commonly extend their shoulder more when throwing a backfist than boxers do when placing a jab.

The backfist is as safe a technique to use as any because you do not have to turn your body to use it. You are in less danger because you reach out with it rather than cross over, and your shoulder and back

This backfist is almost the same exact movement as a boxer's jab.

hand are in place to protect you from a counterstrike.

The backfist has power, but you do not need much power to get the point in a traditional karate tournament. In many cases you will actually lose the point if you use much force.

You can even throw your backfist with an open hand. Keeping your hand open makes the movement faster and gives you three or four extra inches of reach. Your safety mitts make it virtually impossible for the judges to see that your hand is not clenched. You will get more points when you use it, and your opponent will get fewer bruises.

The traditional backfist still has some value as a tournament technique. Use it at events that allow no face contact but do permit hitting to the side of the head. The 35-degree angle of the traditional technique will allow you to hit the side of your opponent's head without getting disqualified for face contact.

Turner faces Kenny Street (above left) and spins around (below left) to deliver a powerful spinning backfist (above).

There is one other type of backfist, but it is not a common tournament technique. It is the spinning backfist and it has two great disadvantages. First, it is slow and requires you to turn your back on your opponent. Second, it is often penalized by judges who consider it to be a blind technique.

A blind technique is any strike that is thrown blind. Close your eyes and punch—that is technically a blind technique. If you use the spinning backfist you must take great care to spin your head around fast enough to gain a view of your opponent before you release the technique. You can expect to get called on this sometimes even if you do not throw it blind.

Do not discount the spinning backfist. It can be used to bridge the gap very effectively if it is done quickly along the direct angle of attack.

Turner demonstrates a blind backfist. Blind techniques of any kind are illegal in most tournaments.

Using the Backfist

I was very successful with the backfist. Often I attacked my opponents several times in a row with a lunging backfist. Whether I got the point or not, I made my opponent bring her hands high and forced her to defend against this very quick technique.

As soon as I felt that I had my opponent conditioned to expect my backfist I would punish her low with a spinning backkick or a quick sidekick. This simple high/low strategy worked to help me win lots of tournaments.

Bruce Lee had a name for this method. He called it half commitment. Your opponent is conditioned to become preoccupied with an attack that will not happen. You make him anticipate a punch that is not really coming, and then you fold him with the real thing.

Howard Jackson and Joe Lewis were both exceptionally good with the backfist. Lewis used it to bridge the gap—to cover up the fact that he was coming after you with a sidekick. He threw his powerful backfist as he stepped forward. The backfist covered his advancing footwork and drew his opponent's eyes upward. Once inside, he fired his sidekick. His backfist fakes were so realistic and so fast that his opponents seldom knew what hit them when the sidekick landed in their ribs.

Lewis was a master of the indirect angle of attack. He used fakes that threw off his opponent's timing and balance. The instant the guy hesitated or broke his rhythm, Lewis would lunge in and hit him with the backfist. His indirect angle of attack caused his opponent to stumble and lose his point of reference. Lewis would blast him with the backfist while his mind was in a state of confusion and his body was half committed.

Lewis was known to say, "If your opponent is faster than you, the indirect angle of attack is the equalizer." He wrote articles on the subject. You might say the indirect angle of attack was his specialty.

Jackson relied heavily on the backfist mostly in conjunction with a direct attack. When the referee said go, Jackson leaped forward, slamming his backfist into the face of his victim. On his second attack Jackson would fake to the head with his backfist, drive home his point with a powerful reverse punch, and then throw another lightning backfist.

Jackson also used his backfist as a defensive move. Rather than step away from his opponent he would step forward at a 45-degree angle. He pushed into his opponents and extended his backfist to catch them halfway into their attack. Jackson's opponent would barely have time to lift a knee before he had a backfist in his face.

Many times I got points against fighters who charged me simply by sticking my backfist out and letting them run into it. By using their momentum and adjusting to their timing I got points without actually doing anything.

By the time I made my first appearance at the Battle of Atlanta I was so excited about the flexibility of the backfist that I based much of my fighting strategy on its limitless potential. My method was simple and with it I won the tournament. In the last part of the final bout I stepped forward from the line and threw a backfist as fast as I could. When my opponent brought her hands up, I nailed her in the gut with a roundkick.

The final point came when I faked a roundkick by thrusting my hip forward. My opponent's hands dropped to cover her now tender midsection. Instantly I pushed off again to cross her critical-distance line. I reached right over the top of her guard and popped her in the jaw with my backfist to earn the winning point.

The backfist is an excellent offensive technique. But I hope that you will stop thinking of it as a technique and instead think in terms of the principles. If you fail to score with your offensive backfist do not give up on the technique. Instead apply the various principles until you unlock the strategy combination that will thwart your opponent's defense.

Perhaps you are up against an opponent who is much faster than you are. If after trying several of the winning principles to your offensive backfist you are still unable to score, simply switch to defense. Take a half step forward at a 45-degree angle and blast him as he starts his run, or take a half step back and plant one on him as he rushes you.

By extending your shoulder and opening your hand you get maximum reach with your backfist. As I said, it is one of the safest techniques you have. Do not, however, drop your guard when you execute a backfist. Remember to keep your back hand high, ready to protect. And be sure to return your backfist to its ready position after each strike. If you extend the punch and leave it out there, your opponent will rush through the opening and smash your face.

Speed comes from relaxation. Keep your body relaxed and both feet on the floor. Throw your backfist with your knees bent and your body aligned.

Because it is the fastest technique you have, you can use your backfist to catch a charger, a blocker, a runner, or an elusive runner. You will get your point when you have bridged the gap and placed your backfist in his face. If he manages to protect his head with a parry, it may be time to stun him with a powerful reverse punch.

The Reverse Punch

If you are a student of a traditional martial art system you probably learned to throw your reverse punch with a great deal of power but with very little regard for defensive positioning. The traditional reverse punch is performed by placing the fist, palm up, at waist level. The elbow stays in as the fist slides forward. Near the end of the blow the fist turns over, creating a corkscrew action intended to accelerate the blow and increase the destruction. At the point in which the tradi-

Karate champion Jim Butin demonstrates the reverse punch.

tional reverse punch is fully extended, the arm will be locked out and the shoulders will be square to the opponent. For tournament competition you have to make some modifications in the traditional method.

Begin by testing the reach of your traditional reverse punch. Face a wall and assume a traditional fighting posture. Now slowly extend your punch. Take notice of how much reach you have.

Now try the same technique, only this time twist your waist. You will find that you have got far greater reach when you add body torque to the technique. Try it on your heavy bag and you will also discover that you have considerably more power with the modern reverse punching method.

Now try the technique again, but this time begin your punch from a point just in front of your chin. As soon as you reach full extension, return the punch to its starting position. Now you have full power, maximum reach, and the best defensive position possible.

It may seem as if I am describing a boxer's right cross. True—the modern version of the reverse punch and the boxer's cross have a lot in common. But there are two differences. First, the karate fist has more

Turner slides under Street's attacking arm and lands a reverse punch. At most upper belt events there is no rule that limits the power that may be used in a blow to the body.

of a drilling action. Second, the karate reverse punch is used primarily as a body blow while the cross is fired to the head or body.

Boxers use even more body torque with their cross than modern karate fighters use with their reverse punch. The boxer can afford more twisting because he does not have to worry about getting kicked nor does he have to concern himself with covering large distances.

As with all techniques the reverse punch should be delivered from a relaxed posture with the knees bent. Real power and speed come from relaxation. Stay loose until the moment of impact.

My favorite fist is the vertical fist because it has greater power. Experiment with both vertical and horizontal fist positions to find which works best for you.

At close range the reverse punch impacts with the palm up. A short-distance reverse punch is similar to an uppercut. It is powerful and extremely difficult to parry.

When to Use the Reverse Punch

It is easy for your opponent to see your reverse punch as it begins its trajectory and crosses over his critical-distance line. If you lead with a reverse punch, your opponent will easily evade you. If you are up against a runner or a blocker, you can't get him with a reverse punch.

Use the reverse punch in conjunction with a fake or an offensive move. Cover by throwing your backfist or your lead-leg sidekick. Distract your opponent to create the opening and gain the time needed to land this powerful punch.

Turner throws a reverse punch without twisting her waist.

The Offensive Reverse Punch

It is not easy but you can use a reverse punch as the first technique if you are fighting a charger. Push into him as he begins to move and

By twisting her waist Turner adds several inches to her reach and unleashes the tremendous power that comes from twisting the body with the punch.

land your reverse punch in his gut as he begins his forward motion. Get as much reach out of the technique as possible by turning your shoulder and torquing your hips. Keep your entire body centered and your head in line with your body. Give yourself a good push with your back leg.

It is very difficult to use the reverse punch offensively because you must generate torque while moving forward, but Howard Jackson was one who could do it well. Because of his excellent balance and the fact that he kept his body perfectly centered, Jackson could use his reverse punch to disable even the fastest of chargers.

Very few fighters know how to punch to the body effectively. Most tournament fighters are head hunters. Their time and energy is spent searching for the head shot. Since most competitors are not able to use the reverse punch, they are not able to defend against it. Many are unfamiliar with the extreme pain that this technique can inflict.

Power Punches

There is no rule that limits the power that may be used in a blow to the body. No matter how hard you slam your reverse punch into your opponent's gut you cannot be disqualified. Therefore you can use your reverse punch to damage your opponent and limit his ability to out-score you.

Fred Wren was a master of the defensive reverse punch. He was a blocker. His strategy was to step back, block the attack, and then let loose with his brutally powerful reverse punch. He routinely hurt his opponents so badly that they were unable to defend.

I use the reverse punch primarily as a defensive technique. If I were up against an especially fast and powerful opponent, I would fade back and fire my reverse punch. I have hit opponents as hard as I could on the initial move. My intent was to cause some pain, to slow them down, and to make them gun-shy.

I remember an incident at Pat Burlson's Fort Worth tournament. My opponent was rushing in on me, and I was using the lunging backfist as a defensive move. She was a large woman, a quick and aggressive charger, so I stood my ground and threw my backfist out as she moved forward. Twice she ran into my backfist. The look in her eye and the language of her body told me that she had my strategy wired. This time she held her hand high to protect against my jamming backfist. Instead of standing there and sticking out my backfist again, I lunged forward and hit her in the body with a solid reverse punch. Her eyes rolled from pain and shock.

In the next round I faced an even bigger woman. She was a charger and very fast for her size. After absorbing a couple of her bruising blows, I realized that I had to hurt her to slow her down and stop her from running over me. The next time off the line I lunged into her, faked a backfist, and then popped her in the solar plexus with a reverse punch. Fear motivated me to hit her as hard as I possibly could. The impact was stunning and her gasp told me I had achieved my goal.

The next point was easy. As she stepped forward I glanced at her rib cage and faked with my right shoulder. Her hands dropped into position to defend against another painful reverse punch. I hit her in the head with a backfist.

Use your reverse punch. It is a valuable part of your arsenal. Apply faking, footwork, and spontaneous combinations to get inside with this powerful punch.

The Sidekick

I love the sidekick! It offers maximum power and maximum reach.

Traditional instructors demand that their students perform all techniques, including the sidekick, exactly as they do. Try as you might, it is unlikely that your sidekick will ever look just like your teacher's. Everyone seems to do this technique a little bit differently. Hip structure, flexibility, and leg build all play a big part.

To achieve a sidekick some people must roll their hip over and practically turn their backside into the kick. Others must throw their sidekick straight from the hip.

The sidekick is very difficult to classify as "right" or "wrong." Test

Turner chambers her leg (lifts her knee), ready to deliver a sidekick.

yourself by the amount of stability, speed, and power that you are able to generate. What matters is whether you can make it work and whether you can avoid having it jammed.

The Skipping Sidekick

Take a left-lead fighting stance. Push forward with your back leg and simultaneously lift your left knee. Draw your knee high and pull it close to your body. Sight the target with your knee, and then unfold your left leg. The kick explodes forward at the instant the support foot lands.

Throw the kick. Make sure your body stays upright but turn your hips slightly to the right. Drive your heel into the target and straighten your leg completely to gain follow-through. For thrusting power, press forward with your body. For snapping power, rechamber the kick.

Turner plants a powerful sidekick.

Joe Lewis never snapped his sidekicks back. Instead he slammed his powerful sidekick into his opponent with full thrust and little or no recoil. The effect was a solid thump. Bill Wallace's method was to strike with the sidekick and return the leg with a snap. The effect was whiplike.

Those who favor the driving-style sidekick brag about its wall-smashing power. Those who prefer to snap their sidekicks say that their method has plenty of power and lets them recover quickly and throw a second technique more rapidly.

Which method is best? Why not do both? Howard Jackson routinely confused his rivals by using both the snapping- and driving-style sidekicks.

Always keep your knees bent. You cannot easily be knocked over or away if you keep your body low by bending your knees. When a fighter straightens his support leg and thrusts his sidekick into an opponent, he may find himself bouncing off his opponent. What should have been a point is lost because of his imbalance and lack of focused power.

When a fighter locks out his support leg and rises up on his toes, he is asking for a fall. In this extended position a good wind could knock him over.

The heavy bag is the best tool for stabilizing your sidekick. Swing it away from you. As it comes toward you, lift your knee and throw your sidekick. If the bag stops dead center, then you know your technique is effective. If you go flying back, you need more bend in your knees and perhaps an adjustment of your body position.

The Secret of the Sidekick

The secret of an effective sidekick is in the position of the knee. Against a heavy bag you will find that you can get quite a lot of power without lifting your knee high. In the ring, however, you will find that the same kick gets jammed. A low chamber (kicking with the knee low) may seem faster, but it will fail you in competition. You must lift your knee high. Otherwise your kick will get snagged both by intentional jams from your opponent and accidental jams as you bang your knee against his.

Use the Sidekick Offensively

The skipping sidekick is extremely versatile because it is a front-leg technique and relatively safe to use. But do not kid yourself; a kick is never as fast as a punch. Although your leg is longer than your arm, it is not the closest weapon to your opponent. A backfist can beat a skipping sidekick every time.

Even Bill Wallace, whose sidekicks were said to be the fastest in the world (up to 60 miles an hour), could not outspeed fast punchers with his super kicks. Wallace and other successful sidekickers used faking and angle of attack to create an opening for this devastating technique.

I used a backfist/sidekick combination with great success. To cover distance I might charge forward with a sidekick and then land a backfist to the head. More often I used my skipping sidekick after a backfist fake. My backfist covered the telegraphing motions of my kick. Before my opponent could recover from the backfist fake, I nailed her with my sidekick.

Use the Sidekick Defensively

What better way to keep a charger at bay than to jam him with a sidekick? As the fool rushes in, lift your knee high and extend the kick. With luck you will get a point. At worst you will keep him away and gain time for a counter.

Whether using your sidekick defensively or offensively, you should never drop your lead hand. Hold your lead hand high or you will find a fist in your face should you miss your target. Conversely, look for fighters who drop their lead hand when they throw a sidekick. Time your counterattack to exploit this opening.

In his early days Bill Wallace deliberately fought with his lead hand low. His strategy was to draw his opponent into range and then crush him with rapid-fire side-, round-, and hookkicks. It worked for Wallace because with his strength and balance he could avoid incoming punches by leaning backward.

Obviously there are few fighters with the ability to stand on one leg and lean their body out of the range of all incoming punches and kicks. Keep your guard high.

Sidekick Strategies

Telegraphing is the Achilles' heel of the sidekick. Try as you might you cannot completely avoid telegraphing your intent with this technique. You can always cover by faking, and you can use Principle 11, Reach; bridge the gap with hyperextension and double hyperextension.

When you lift your knee for a sidekick your opponent will realize that a kick is coming and react accordingly. The chances are good that he will step away from your kick to a range just beyond the extension of your limb. This is when you nail him with hyperextension.

Instead of just stepping forward and throwing the sidekick with your lead leg, slide into the technique. Your slide will add another 12 to 24 inches of reach to your kick. That is a foot or two that he will not expect.

If he gets away from your hyperextension kick, you can knock him right out of the ring with double hyperextension. Step first, slide, and then kick while you slide again. With this combination of forward stepping and quick sliding, you can cover as much as eight feet with your lead-leg sidekick.

Eight feet will get you where you need to be. Remember there is not much room for him to run from you in a karate ring. Who can escape from a fighter capable of spanning eight feet in a split second?

Apply hyper- and double hyperextension to your lead-leg sidekicks and to other techniques to close the gap and cover the distance between yourself and your opponent. With Principle 11, Reach, you should never need more than two moves to connect with your opponent.

Sidekicks hurt and your opponent knows it. Even veteran fighters fear it. Because of its reputation the sidekick makes an especially good fake. Simply by shifting your hip you can draw your opponent's attention to his midsection. As he drops his guard, blast him with a head or upperbody technique.

You can use your sidekick with combinations of techniques. The idea is to harass him while keeping him away from your critical-distance line.

For those hard-to-tag opponents, you may wish to apply angle of attack. If he is a charger, step 45 degrees to the side and then throw your sidekick. If he is extremely fast, step 45 degrees to the rear and throw your kick.

If you face a fast charger, step away from him several times in a row. When you see that he has caught on to the timing, step forward. Push into him with your lunging sidekick—you will love the look on his face when he runs into your most powerful kick.

Use your sidekick to jam your opponent's kicks. Lift your knee and extend your kick until your foot touches your opponent's kicking leg.

Your leg-checking technique will thwart his kick and may toss him off balance, leaving him open to your next attack.

Leg checks are one of the best ways to stop a frequent kicker like champion George Chung. Chung would hop forward on one leg and kick with relentless vigor. Leg checks might have been the only way to stop Chung.

Leg checks are worth doing only if you follow them with an immediate attack. Make sure that your leg check stays in place until you counter or your frequent kicker will escape the check and punish you for your efforts.

Bill Wallace was an expert at the sidekick/leg check. He would check his opponent's kick and hold it until the man dropped his guard. Then without lowering his checking leg he would kick again. His strategy was to check low and then kick high. He is the unquestioned master of this technique. After twenty years I still get goosebumps when I watch him perform his double, triple, and quadruple kicking and checking combinations.

The Rear-Leg Sidekick

The lead-leg sidekick is the primary technique and the one that works best for tournaments. The rear-leg sidekick has power, but it is seldom used to good effect in a tournament match.

In order to throw the rear-leg sidekick you must lift your knee in a relatively wide arc. At the same time you must turn your body 180 degrees. There is simply too much telegraphing for this kick to have much use in the high-speed world of tournament fighting.

Understanding Straight Kicks

Mechanically the frontkick is very similar to the sidekick. Both are straight-line kicks and both afford the attacker considerable power and reach. The frontkick is quicker than the sidekick and easier to execute. At first glance the frontkick looks like the best straight-line kick. In some styles, Thai boxing comes to mind, the sidekick is avoided altogether in favor of the frontkick.

In the West, tournament fighters consistently favor the sidekick over the frontkick as the straight-line kick of choice. To throw a frontkick you must square your body to your opponent and expose the entire

Turner faces her opponent (see next page).

front of your body with its many legal target points. It is a risky thing to do. In contrast the sidekick gives you maximum protection while affording you the many benefits of a straight-line kick.

Use your sidekick liberally and your frontkick very sparingly. Side-kicks win tournaments.

Roundkick

A tournament-style karate roundkick is delivered with the front leg. It is done in exactly the same way that a sidekick is delivered, with the knee high and the foot close to the body. Once again Bill Wallace is the one to emulate. He throws his stunning roundkick from exactly the same starting position as he does his sidekick. Until the moment of impact his side-, round-, and hookkicks are indistinguishable.

Turner slides forward to land a front-leg roundkick.

Even today Bill Wallace still throws the best roundkick I've seen. His flexibility and agility are wonderful. He raises his knee so high that he can hit his opponent anywhere he wants. His ability is such that he can stand on one leg and comb his hair with his toes. I've seen him conduct an interview while standing on one leg with his roundhouse kick fully extended and pointing at the interviewer. He has held his leg extended for five to ten minutes.

Wallace uses his knee to aim his roundkick at the target. As it does for the sidekick, the knee acts as the scope from which to aim and throw the roundkick. Point your knee at your target and then extend your roundkick. Always start the technique with your knee held high or else you will lack power and accuracy.

Hold your body upright as you kick. Otherwise you cannot follow your roundkick with additional advancing techniques.

Targets and Strategies for the Roundkick

The best target for the roundkick is the midsection. The second best target is your opponent's head. Confuse your opponent by kicking him with high and low combinations.

Use your backfist to draw your opponent's guard high, and then slam your roundhouse kick into his body. Even if he manages to lower his arms in time to block your roundkick, you will plant the seed of doubt in his mind. Next time you charge, fake to the body and roundkick high to his head.

Rear-Leg Roundkicks

Even Wallace admits that he cannot get the power with a lead-leg roundkick as he can with a rear-leg kick. There is substantially less power to be had when kicking with the lead leg. Wallace says power was never a problem.

"It was never stated that I had to hit hard [to get the point]," Wallace says. "All I had to do was hit close with a good strong technique."

The leadside roundkick is a point-getter and a very effective tournament technique. The back-leg roundkick is surprisingly fast. Like the rear-leg sidekick the back-leg roundkick must come from behind and arc up. It swings into the target. But tests indicate that it is much faster than the rear-leg sidekick and telegraphs less.

The back-leg roundkick is a power hitter. Use it offensively and defensively as you use your reverse punch. Create an opening with your initial move, and then fire your back-leg roundkick into the unguarded area.

The Roundkick on Defense

The roundkick is a great defensive technique. To defend against a charger, step straight to the side and counterattack with your roundhouse. Move to a 45-degree angle and kick. You cannot miss. Step to your opponent's back side.

If your roundkick keeps getting blocked, change your angle of attack. Before my hand techniques were fully developed I fought a woman whose expertise was in defending against kicks. Try as I might I could not get my roundkick in because of her excellent blocks.

On impulse I changed my angle of attack. With footwork I gained position to throw my back-leg roundkick. Instead of bringing it straight around at knee level as I had been doing, I brought it under her defenses. It was almost a straight-legged movement. My leg traveled right under her block and into her midsection.

The Roundkick on Offense

If you are very quick you can use your front-leg roundkick to attack your opponent on your initial move. The roundkick is quicker than the sidekick and may therefore be launched with less warning. To make it work you must lift your knee at the same instant you push off with your rear leg. Release the kick with an explosive snap.

If you are a bit slow, fake with your backfist or use another upper-body technique. When his hands rise, thump him with your snapping roundkick. The roundkick can be used on all angles of attack—inside, middle, and outside. From the lead side it can be used to bridge the gap with a lunge. It works on a curved line as a defensive back-leg kick.

Practice the roundkick from a moving position. Use footwork to set up your technique because it adds speed and makes it hard for your opponent to guess your intent.

The roundkick is very effective in combinations against an elusive runner. Throw roundkicks and punches so quickly that he does not have time to plant and counter.

Faking works well, too. It was my favorite because I was very fast with the initial move. I have hit an opponent with the lunging round, and then I have used it as a fake. Lunge with your lead side. Use your hip and make him jump. Do not extend your leg. Just step down and come in with a high kick or a backfist.

Against a charger use direct angle of attack on the initial move. You have got to move before he moves or move in to draw him out. When he charges, go back into him and hit him with your lunging roundkick. Hit him between moves.

Against a blocker use angles of attack. Throw one technique, and then push off at a 45-degree angle to attack his back side. Throw off his timing by throwing the technique above his guard one time, and then do it again with a hesitation that draws his counter. Hit him low at that instant. Throw your roundkick underneath his guard.

If you are terribly slow, give up on the offensive roundkick. Substitute hand attacks and save your roundkick for defensive counterattacks.

The Backkick and Spinning Backkick

Here is a surprise: the backkick is one of karate's fastest kicks. Although I rarely used it in tournaments I have great respect for this excellent technique.

By definition a tournament-style backkick is like a sidekick except that the back faces the opponent. The backkick is like its name. To try it out just put yourself in a position with your back to your opponent, and then kick him as a mule would kick. The support foot is planted with its toes pointed directly away from the target, and the kicker sights his opponent by looking over his own shoulder.The backkick is the leg equivalent of a full-power reverse punch to the body.

The backkick works well against the body's midsection. If you throw it straight it has maximum power and will give your opponent a tremendous and immediate bellyache. If you try for a high strike and throw your backkick at a rising angle, then you are going to have to lean your body and you will lose the ability to push off with your next technique.

Jim Butin was an excellent backkicker. He used deception to fool his opponent into thinking that he was moving away when in fact he was about to move forward.

Says Butin: "I based the timing for my backkick on the initial movement of my opponent. I gave him an opening for a roundkick by holding my hand very high. When I saw his rear foot slide forward I knew he was coming. That first indication of motion was my key to spin around and throw my turning backkick.

"Once he started moving in on an attack he was committed to continue moving in that way. When he picked up his foot to begin his step, there was no turning back. He could not stop in midair. He has no choice but to come forward, right into my spinning backkick."

Butin's defensive backkick was punishing. The angle of his kick was very straight, making it almost impossible to escape. According to Butin: "If he tried to block, I kicked him in his shoulder or hip. If he did not block I hit him in the body. It was a no-lose deal—I landed my backkick somewhere."

The spinning and jump-spinning versions of the backkick require the fighter to spin 360 degrees. The power that results from this full-body torque is tremendous. Spinning the body also tends to confuse the defender and thereby expose openings in his defense.

The spinning backkick is closely related to the sidekick. Instead of skipping forward and kicking, the backkicker spins in place and fires the kick at the end of the turn.

Drawbacks

Like all techniques the backkick has its drawbacks. To use it you must turn your back to your opponent, which may subject you to counterattack. If you spin with the technique you gain the advantage of even more power, but you risk getting clobbered because you have turned your back and lost sight of him for part of a second. Whether you launch your backkick with a step, a spin, or a jump spin, you will land in a position that affords few opportunities for follow-up techniques.

The turning backkick can be used with offensive combinations but its best use is on defense. "The turning backkick is very hard to use offensively," says Butin.

More Ways to Use the Backkick

The backkick has knockout power. A backkick to the center of the body can generate the hurt necessary to slow down a feisty opponent. A direct hit to the body below the ribs can create a "body knockout" by shocking the liver.

Use this powerful technique anytime you are up against a bigger and stronger adversary. Your well-placed backkick can cripple his ability to storm you by taking away his wind and replacing it with fear.

You can backkick your way out of trouble if you are up against a particularly aggressive charger. Take a half step backward and then throw your backkick into his path. You will stop him cold.

Training the Backkick

The turning backkick is the most difficult of the primary kicks. It takes months and sometimes years to get this valuable technique under control. Unfortunately most fighters develop their backkick only on one side. Consequently their ability to apply the 18 Principles to this excellent technique is limited by half.

Train both sides of your body equally in this and all of the primary techniques. To overcome the natural laziness of your weaker side, train your weak side twice as hard as you train your more powerful side. Continue to push your weak side until you bring it up to speed with your strong side.

If you stay with it you will be amazed to discover that your weaker side will ultimately have greater power than your strong side. It is amazing but you may even end up with twice the power from your "weaker" side. This is one of the phenomena of karate training. Your well-trained "weak" side will be less restricted by your conscious mind. It will be faster, slightly less controlled, and it will have a much quicker reflex response than your "strong" side.

I trained myself in the use of the backkick and the other primary techniques by limiting myself to one technique at a time. I sparred with multiple opponents, but I restricted myself to the use of only one technique.

It is one thing to be able to defeat your sparring partner with the use of your full repertoire of weapons; it is another thing to beat your training opponent with only one technique. My intention was to force myself to apply as many of the principles to that one technique as possible.

When you can win against your training partners with only one technique, then you know that your faking is solid. You have no doubt that your ability to use angle of attack or any of the other principles is complete. By doing this you also give yourself maximum training on your backkick, or whichever primary technique you have chosen for your drill on that particular day.

5,000 Possibilities

When Bruce Lee identified the five primary techniques, it is a sure bet that he did not expect the martial arts world to abandon the million and one other techniques that are available in karate. There are plenty of solid and legal karate techniques for you to work with if you choose. The wisdom of Lee's theory of the five primary techniques is in the fact that all complexities evolve from the basics and that the use of the 18 Principles creates a plethora of opportunities for these proven standards.

If the number five seems small to you, consider this mathematical fact. Five times 18—primary techniques multiplied by 18 Principles—is equal to 90 different versions of these basic techniques. Those 90 versions further multiplied by the limitless numbers of combinations of the 18 Principles equal thousands upon thousands of strategic possibilities and methods to which the basics can be applied.

5
Strategies for Tournament Fighting

Thereare can be no discussion of strategy without a discussion of the principles that make the strategies work. Speaking of strategy without the principles is like taking a flower apart and examining it under a microscope. You may learn some things about cell structure but you destroy the flower in the process.

Before we can employ any combat strategy we must first have a working understanding of the winning principles. We must realize that those principles, like the art of war so well understood by Sun Tzu in the fourth century B.C., have infinite flexibility.

Sun Tzu said: "The musical notes are only five in number but their melodies are so numerous that one cannot hear them all. The primary colors are only five in number but their combinations are so infinite that one cannot visualize them all. The flavors are only five in number but their blends are so various that one cannot taste them all."

The same is true in karate and in war. Although you may use as few as five techniques, you will be perceived by your enemy as using countless numbers of fighting strategies. By using the 18 Principles your strategies will multiply into an array of possibilities so complex that no one will be able to defend against you.

Setup Strategies

To win one hundred victories in one hundred battles is not the acme of skill; to subdue the enemy without fighting is the acme of skill.
                                                —Sun Tzu, *The Art of War*

Setups have two stages. The first is what you do before a fight to intimidate or fool your opponent. The second stage is what you do that may mislead your opponent as to your intent or your ability before you come off the line.

Karate champions Joe Lewis and Jim Harrison were masters at intimidating their opponents before fights. But tournament winner Jim Butin looked anything but mean. In contrast to Lewis or Harrison he seemed an easy mark.

"I think people would look at me and say, 'I want him; I can take him,'" Butin remembered. "If anything, my body language told people to come on and get me."

Part of his problem was size. "I was six feet, two inches, 155 pounds when I made black belt," he said. "Because I was tall I had to fight heavyweights. Those guys were 222 to 240 pounds and mean. When they grabbed me and hit me just one time, I was hurt."

Butin learned fast that the only way he could survive the circuit was to outsmart his larger adversaries. He decided to put his nice guy image to work for himself rather than let it continue to work against him. Instead of trying to intimidate his opponents before a fight, he acted natural, which is to say he acted the part of an easy mark, a pushover.

"It worked," he said. "People thought I was easy. When they got into the ring with me they quickly learned the truth. Most of the time I was the one who won."

While he was playing his nice guy part he watched and analyzed his opponents. "If you are serious about becoming a champion, you have to watch the people you will be fighting," he said. "Watch the punches and kicks. Look for the telltale movement that telegraphs intent. When you get into the ring you will have the clues you need to pull the trigger. Find ways to read your opponent before you fight him; then you will have time to develop a strategy that will destroy him."

Subdue Without Fighting

Your prefight strategy is every bit as important as your combat strategy. Butin remembered a time when he walked away from a match rather than fight master intimidator Fred Wren.

"It was 1968 just after I made black belt and Fred Wren was already the terror of black belt competition in Dallas and the rest of Texas. Fred was not content with winning a match by scoring more points than the other guy. He made it clear that he was there to beat the stuffings out of his opponent. Wren intimidated people by not talking to anyone and by pacing the floor with an intense look on his face. I had the feeling that his plan was to punish anyone who got in front of him and to hurt anyone who got between him and first place. In the ring he was an extremely physical fighter. He pushed his opponent around and knocked him around and then stared at him as if to say, 'What are you going to do about it?'

"I had watched Wren beat up a lot of guys. His fighting method was to grab your sleeve, roundkick, and punch as hard as he could. He came in so hard and so fast that you could not possibly block all of his strikes. Wren did not have that much variety but what he did, he did well and with tremendous violent energy. I knew I did not want any part of that guy."

The pressure was too much for the young Butin. Here is how it happened. "I was there," he said. "I showed up for the bout but I did not fight Wren—I was too psyched out." A humiliated Jim Butin walked away from the fight that day.

This was the first of several such experiences for the young black belt. His ego was bruised by Wren's powerful prefight psych game, but his spirit was far from beaten.

"I was determined after that bad night that I would never walk away from a match again no matter how terrified I might be. I vowed that I would get back into the ring with Wren and fight," Butin said.

It was not long until Butin drew Fred Wren again. Although he was still intimidated by the man, he stayed for the fight. Chuck Norris was the center referee and he had his hands full because it was a wild fight.

"I finally won the match on points but Fred beat the powder out of me. He threw me on the floor, stomped on me, and dragged me around. He kicked me while I was down. He did everything he could do before Norris could get him off me. I won the match and he won the war. It was a terrible struggle," Butin said.

Fred Wren quickly proved how much he hated to lose. After this second fight with Butin his psych game turned really brutal. The message that came by way of karate rumor was clear and simple—Fred Wren was going to annihilate Jim Butin the next time he got into the ring with him.

"I learned from a friend that Wren had my picture on his heavy bag.

I heard that he was making all of his sparring partners fight like I fought and that all he talked about was beating me," Butin said.

The next tournament was at Dallas and Wren was there. His eyes were daggers staring Butin down. "I wanted to tell him it is only a game—it's not life or death," Butin said. He felt his nerve slipping away as he tried to hold up to Wren's "evil eye." "I kept hoping that he would get eliminated or that I would get eliminated. Finally it got down to four guys, Wren, Harold Gross, another Dallas fighter, and me.

"Before we fought, Harold Gross said, 'Jim, you had better let me win because Wren is going to tear your a—— up.' Gross was a friend and I believe that he was honestly concerned about me. My stomach tied itself into knots."

In spite of his fear Butin fought hard and won the match with Gross anyway. By the time he stepped into the ring with Wren his self-confidence was so wobbly that he had virtually no chance of winning.

"I was so psyched out that I felt like life as I knew it was over. This was death time. I felt that there was no way I could win," Butin recalled. "I was sure that if I survived at all it would be hospitalization, tubes, and catheters."

When at last the moment of truth came Butin's nerve was shattered. "I got up there with him and I threw a few half-hearted techniques. Wren won handily but he did not hurt me," Butin said. Butin was relieved that he escaped undamaged. He was so happy to have survived that he forgot to be unhappy about losing.

"The next day I analyzed what happened. I realized that I was my own worst enemy—that Wren beat me long before I ever stepped into the ring. I knew that if I was to continue I could never let myself be psyched out like that again."

Fortunately for Butin he learned his hard lesson about prefight psych-outs at an early stage in his career. "I was only 18 or 19 at the time," he said. "That is when I had my 'Fred Wren,' as I used to call it. It was a major growth step for me and a turning point in my career."

Butin fought Fred Wren two times after the Dallas event. He says their next match was a real fight. "Wren finally won but I dropped him with a turnkick. I felt great because I really fought him." The last time Butin fought Wren, Butin won.

Joe Lewis was also a master of setting up his opponent through intimidation. Butin remembered meeting Lewis for the first time: "Joe Lewis was talking with promoter Mike Anderson but he was looking at me. I could feel his eyes burning into mine. He stared at me hard. I believe he did this to see if I would return his stare or turn away from him or what. I was very uncomfortable. He was very strong and very intimidating."

What happens inside your head before you ever step into the ring will make you or break you. Never underestimate the power of the prefight setup.

Like Fred Wren and Joe Lewis you can begin setting your opponent up with intimidation tactics long before you actually fight. Or like Jim Butin and Howard Jackson you can play it easy and mislead your opponent until the fight begins. You should continue to set your opponent up before you begin each individual attack by using eye contact, body language, and the other techniques that have been described.

Strategies Using Positioning

The experts in defense conceal themselves as under the ninefold earth; those skilled in attack move as from above the ninefold heavens; thus they are capable both of protecting themselves and of gaining a complete victory.

—Sun Tzu, *The Art of War*

A general knows that victory can be attained only if his army achieves superior positioning on the field of battle. He moves his troops to high ground, places them with the sun at their back, and maneuvers them continually to ensure that he maintains this superior position.

Karate fighters do the same thing. Already you have learned the importance of positioning yourself in relation to the referee's view. Once the battle is engaged, you must also vie for superior position in a constantly moving scenario. Both you and your opponent seek superior position from which to launch your attack.

If you cannot achieve a position inside his critical-distance line you cannot hit him. If you are able to get inside but unable to do so without losing your balance, you have gained no advantage.

You do not want your opponent to know where you are headed any more than you want him to know what you are going to do when you get there. Your body language can give away your positioning strategy just as it can give away your attack strategy. Execute your footwork maneuvers so that you do not telegraph. Experiment with active and passive body language to fool your opponent into thinking that you are about to do something that you are not about to do.

Always position yourself with mobility in mind. Remember fighting is about moving. Move defensively and offensively at 45 degree angles and attain the superior positioning you need to score your point. Keep your knees bent as you move and keep your body centered.

Kick and punch from a mobile position rather than a static one. You will be faster and harder to stop if you strike from a moving position. Remember to move with your weight on your toes rather than trying to gain position from a cold, flat-footed posture.

Do not rise up too high on the balls of your feet, and do not lean too far forward or backward. Leaning forward or backward, especially with kicks, will limit your power and open your body to counterattack. Test yourself regularly by watching yourself in a mirror, by asking someone to watch you, and by videotaping yourself. If you see that you are landing off balance with any given technique, something is wrong with that maneuver.

Howard Jackson was my role model for combative positioning. He fought with his knees bent and his body centered. He moved side to side just as well and just as quickly as he moved forward. He could

Karyn Turner moving at a 45-degree angle to gain superior positioning and score her point.

retreat with the same efficiency as he advanced. When he moved backward his body was so well centered that he could counter as needed with power and accuracy.

Your best techniques are worthless if you cannot get into position to score with them. Your punches and kicks will do no harm if you attempt to launch them from an inferior position. Position yourself for the best line of attack—inside, outside, indirect, or direct—as the situation dictates. Stay relaxed and explode into the attack.

Positioning is partly mental. Use body language to make your opponent think that you are confident and that you fight from a position of strength. For the skilled fighter, offense blends with defense and vice versa. Defense is not merely a matter of blocking. It includes evading and positioning, striking and counterattacking.

To position yourself for the best defensive capability keep in mind all of your defensive choices. You can block, you can move out of the way, you can jam, and you can block and strike simultaneously.

My defensive reaction time was not as fast as it needed to be. To gain the position I needed to ensure that my defense would work I would move toward the incoming blow. By moving into the attack I increased the effectiveness of my block, reduced the chances that I would be hit and knocked off balance, and simultaneously gained excellent position from which to launch my counterattack.

Strategies Using Independent Movement

His potential is that of a fully drawn crossbow; his timing, the release of the trigger.

—Sun Tzu, *The Art of War*

An independent movement is any movement that can be executed without telegraphing. Independent movement was one of Bruce Lee's great strengths. His speed was so great and his attacks were so unexpected that he could counter his opponent's technique before his opponent could do that technique.

Independent movement is lost anytime you chamber or cock your arm or leg in preparation for an attack. Cocking your arm not only tells your opponent what you are going to do but also opens up your face as a target for him to strike.

Chambering and telegraphing are acts that hint of future actions. By the time you have pulled your hand back the opportunity to punch will be gone.

Turner strikes without warning. An independent movement is any movement that can be executed without telegraphing.

Independent movement is motion without thought. It is an action of the present. The Chinese call it the "no mind" state. Independent movement comes only when a technique is overlearned to the point that it is a natural response to a given opportunity. Like writing your name, scratching your nose, or shaking hands, an independent karate movement is one that is so natural that it is completely free of pre-planned thought.

It is easiest to apply independent movement using lead-side techniques. The backfist is the best technique to use with independent movement because it is a technique that requires no extra motion that might telegraph your intention.

The strategy of independent movement is a "no-strategy strategy." It is the principle of pure motion. Few fighters had as good a grasp of the concept as Howard Jackson.

A number of top fighters learned the secrets of independent movement from Jackson. Jim Butin was already a top contender when he worked out with Jackson. He said Jackson taught him new secrets of unpredictability. "I learned to fire techniques with no telegraphing, no windups, and no unnecessary chambering," he said.

Strategies Using Initial Speed

While we have heard of blundering swiftness in war, we have not yet seen a clever operation that was prolonged. . . . An attack may lack ingenuity, but it must be delivered with supernatural speed.
—Sun Tzu, *The Art of War*

Do you remember in your driver education class when the visiting highway patrolman warned you to stay several car lengths behind the vehicle in front of you? The faster you go the farther back you are supposed to hang—40 miles an hour, four lengths; 50 miles an hour, five lengths, and so on. The reason is reaction time. The faster you go, the less time you have to react to avoid a possible impact.

Bill Wallace's kicks were clocked at 60 miles per hour. Imagine how fast you would have to be to escape his speed. How many "leg lengths" should you stay clear to avoid becoming another superfoot statistic? The kick is coming from a chambered position so it has to travel about three feet. Three feet times 60 miles an hour . . . that gives you about a fraction of a second to get out of harm's way.

The point is that reaction time is much slower than action time. If you cannot outrun an opponent in a fair race, how can you hope to beat him if he has a head start?

He who strikes first has that head start. When Wallace launched his 60-mile-an-hour kick his opponent's brain used up most of its "race" time just in realizing that the kick was coming. This is the essence of initial speed.

Initial speed is perhaps the most important of the 18 Principles. Used in conjunction with independent movement, footwork, and other principles, initial speed is your big gun.

Fighters like Lewis and Jackson used initial speed right off the line and got points on their opponents before their opponents could even move. But they did not stop there. They applied initial speed with each subsequent attack. Both fighters used footwork and positioning to conceal their intent and increase the shock of their initial attacks.

Initial attack is easier to use from a moving position than it is from a stationary place. With footwork you will confuse your opponent. When you launch your initial speed attack while in motion, it is even more difficult for your opponent to detect your intent. His reaction time will be about twice as long as normal.

The backfist in conjunction with initial speed was always my favorite. Wherever I went I used a relaxed-hand backfist to knock points out of my opponents.

Strategies for Attack Lines

Probe him and learn where his strength is abundant and where deficient.

—Sun Tzu, *The Art of War*

The attack lines include the inside line, the middle line, and the outside line. To visualize the outside line imagine that you move toward your opponent's back side at a 45 degree angle. Take the same 45 degree angle—this time moving toward your opponent's stomach—and you will understand the inside line. Picture yourself pushing off straight into your opponent and you have grasped the concept of the middle line.

The three attack lines are vital to any winning strategy. Bill Wallace's single-leg kicking method makes a wonderful example of attack-line strategies. Because he confined his leg attacks to three kicks—the roundhouse, the sidekick, and the hookkick—and his hands mostly to the backfist it is easy to see the application of attack lines in his performance. We will get the best possible description of Wallace's attack-line strategies by examining his fights. For this purpose I have chosen his two fights against rival Jim Butin.

Jim Butin's first fight with Wallace was in 1971, the second in 1973. On both occasions Butin came close to victory, and on the second occasion he blew a substantial lead, missing his last chance to defeat Wallace.

"Each time we fought I went in thinking I could whip him," Butin remarked. Now he believes he lost to Wallace partly because of his own overconfidence and mostly because of Wallace's excellent use of attack-line strategies.

"The first time we fought we went into overtime," he said. "My

Turner attacks her opponent along his inside line.

confidence was high until he hit me with a defensive sidekick along the middle line and knocked the wind out of me. I tried a sweep but he evaded and landed the winning point.

"By the time I got my second shot at him in 1973 I wanted him bad," Butin recalled. "I knew I was ready, and I believed that I could beat him."

Butin got off to a good start. His kicks were effective, and he even managed to sweep Wallace and body-punch him.

"I felt like I was serving up some justice," he said. "He moved in and tried to hit me with a backfist, but I got him again, this time with a roundhouse kick to the face! Suddenly it was 2 to 0 and I only needed three points to win. I thought, 'This is it, I have Bill Wallace!' "

But Wallace came back with a fury. He moved to the outside line and surprised Butin with a tricky and fast backfist. Almost immediately he got a second point on Butin with an inside-line kick, and the score was tied at 2–2. "I was so upset that I had blown my lead that for a moment I did not even know if he had hit me with a roundkick or a hook."

At this point Butin admits that he lost his cool. "I still felt I could win but I wanted a macho victory. I had wanted to beat him 3–0."

Finally the match went into overtime. "I swept him again and hit him with a solid body-punch. At the same time he hit me with an inside-line kick. It was a heelkick right in the sight line of the referee."

Suddenly Butin was lying on the apron. "Someone came over to me and asked me if I was all right." Butin knew that his middle-line reverse punch had landed with a solid thump. Even though he had been knocked off his feet and dazed in the exchange of blows, he could not accept the fact that the judges called Wallace's kick instead of his punch.

"I think I wanted to win so badly that I justified it," he admitted. Dazed from the blow, Butin rose from the apron. He remained convinced that the point should have been his. But in the view of the judges Wallace's inside line-of-attack heelkick had cancelled out Butin's middle-line counterattack. Although both blows happened at the same time the referee and the judges had been able to see only Wallace's inside-line kick while Butin's technique was obscured from their view.

Bill Wallace was a world-class competitor and Butin knew he had reached the big leagues when he came close to winning against "Superfoot."

"As it turned out Wallace won first place each time we fought and I won second. But I had fun fighting him. He was top talent and I knew that it wouldn't be easy for anyone to beat him."

Fighting Wallace only served to enhance Butin's understanding of attack-line strategies. Fueled with this knowledge and ample experience he went on to become a champion fighter in his own right. Later Jim Butin fought as a representative of his country along with Bill Wallace, Jeff Smith, Joe Lewis, Howard Jackson, and me on our European karate tour.

Strategies for Bridging the Gap

When near, make it appear that you are far away; when far away, that you are near.
                                   —Sun Tzu, *The Art of War*

The gap is the distance between you and your opponent. "Bridging the gap" means spanning the distance between you and your opponent's

Karate champion Steve Fisher (left) lunges forward to bridge the gap and gain entry into his opponent's defenses.

critical-distance line—the point at which your opponent can be reached by fist or foot.

Initial speed and footwork bring you to your opponent. Faking, extension, hyperextension, and double hyperextension are what get you inside.

As I have said earlier, the critical-distance line is the point at which you can strike your opponent. Critical distance is further defined as either long-kicking range, kicking range, or punching range.

Long-kicking range is the distance at which you may kick your opponent only with a hop or a slide forward and only with your longest reaching kick. Kicking and punching range is the point at which you may comfortably reach your opponent with your kicks and can also reach him with a punch if you hyper- or double hyperextend. Punching range is the close distance at which punches work best. Punching range is too close for kicks to be used comfortably.

How you maneuver yourself to bridge the gap determines where you arrive in relation to your opponent's critical-distance line. It determines whether you will arrive at the kicking distance or at the punching distance. Your use of footwork determines how you will be positioned when you arrive at the critical-distance line. For instance you might arrive at the critical-distance line appropriate for punching only to find that you are positioned at an angle that prevents you from scoring. Proper application of angle of attack and footwork ensure that you will arrive at the correct distance in the right position to attack.

Strategies Using Simplicity of Technique

When I have won a victory I do not repeat my tactics but respond to circumstances in an infinite variety of ways.
—Sun Tzu, *The Art of War*

Jim Butin had a gift for strategy. He picked techniques that other fighters perceived as too simple or too much trouble to bother with and used them to his advantage.

"The frontkick is very simple, but I noticed that nobody used it in competition," he said. "People preferred to use the sidekick because there was a danger of having your toes jammed with the frontkick. I decided to use it anyway, thinking that defenses would be weak since no one was doing it in competition." It came as a total shock to his opponents. Time after time he stung them with quick and powerful straight frontkicks. This simple technique helped him win many fights.

One day Butin overheard a couple of guys talking about his front-kick. "Watch out for Butin's front-thrust kick," they warned. "It is all he throws." Butin knew that his simple strategy had been discovered. It was time to give them something else.

"I started sweeping," he said. "It was bread and butter, like the frontkick, because is was so simple and because no one was doing it." Butin continued to use his "simplicity and surprise" theory. Next he perfected his defensive turning backkick and got more points the easy way.

When he was in Europe with the team, light heavyweight champion Jeff Smith taught Butin another jewel of simplicity. It was the double-leg takedown.

"When your opponent moves back, just hook his back leg with your front leg and he will fall," Butin explained. "I was so impressed with it I tried it with great success at the Top Ten Nationals in St. Louis shortly after we returned from Europe." As with the frontkick and turning backkick, Butin had discovered another simple technique that few people knew how to defend against.

Surprise your opponent by using techniques he is not familiar with. Watch him in advance to learn his stuff. Then use the simple solutions to beat him.

Simplicity does not always mean variety. Use the principles to convert your standard simple techniques into a thousand variations of the same. Remember the success of Lewis, Wallace, Jackson, and Wren, each of whom propelled himself to stardom with the use of a few simple techniques.

The beauty of an art form is the simplicity of its expression. With a minimum of movement and energy the champion achieves a direct expression of his inner self.

Most of your opponents will try to complicate their karate by overdoing fancy techniques and bogging down in metaphysical distractions. Instead of fighters with heart they are like robots with computer-chip brains. They are static fighters with little or no spontaneous strategy. They are clones of their instructors and seek to reproduce stilted techniques as exactly and as mechanically as possible.

Most of your opponents will stay locked inside this nonexpressive mechanical stage of karate—they will spend years adding as many techniques to their list as possible. Bruce Lee taught that learning to express yourself in fighting is not a process of adding material to the basics on a daily basis. He said that learning to express the martial arts requires a daily decrease, a stripping away of the nonessential. Find your karate truth in simplicity.

Never forget that your karate is an art form. Lee believed that accomplishment in any form of art means a direct and simple expression of how you feel. Just as a painter mixes paints and achieves a unique blend of colors and beauty on his canvas, you must express your karate technique in a unique and personal way. And like Picasso you can most easily achieve the fullest expression of your art and your own inner ability if you stress the simple. The more complex you make your style the less chance you will have for self-expression.

Strategies Using Economy of Motion

When he concentrates, prepare against him; where he is strong, avoid him.

—Sun Tzu, *The Art of War*

As Bruce Lee was fond of reminding us, the shortest distance between two objects is a straight line. Simply put, economy of motion in karate is the easiest and fastest method possible to achieve an objective.

Bruce Lee's original art was wing chun kung fu. One of the corner-stones of the wing chun system is the principle of economy of motion.

In his lifetime Lee extended and elaborated the wing chun tech-niques and theories that he had learned from wing chun master Yip Man. He also absorbed as much wisdom from as many different styles as he possibly could. Although his own personal fighting style changed over the years as he added principles and techniques from other systems, he never forgot about economy of motion.

No matter how many different techniques you maintain in your inventory you should use economy of motion with each one. If, heaven forbid, you use flying sidekicks in the ring, you should learn to do them with the least amount of waste. Economy of motion must be applied to all of your footwork and all of your positioning strategies as well as to every punch, kick, block, and dodge you execute.

Economy of motion reduces telegraphing and increases speed and power. Realizing that straight lines were more economical than curved lines, Bruce Lee relied heavily on straight-line techniques along the direct angle of attack.

Bruce Lee also used more lead-side techniques than he did rear-side maneuvers. Lead-side techniques are more economical than back-side attacks because they are closer to the target and take less time to execute.

In general, techniques you launch from your lead side along the direct line of attack will provide you with the most powerful and efficient route to your opponent. Therefore I recommend that you spend the majority of your practice time perfecting lead-side straight-line techniques and applying to them the principles of initial speed and direct line of attack.

And remember to use economy of motion in everything else you do, too. If you use ridge hands, left hooks, uppercuts, or other circular techniques, seek the most efficient method of application. Use econ-omy of motion in your defense and in your offensive footwork. Do not forget the wisdom of Bruce Lee: economize your every move.

Strategies Using Relaxation

An army may be likened to water for just as flowing water avoids the heights and hastens to the lowlands, so an army avoids strength and strikes weakness.

—Sun Tzu, *The Art of War*

Bruce Lee recommended that students stay relaxed at all times, using strength only as the situation required. He insisted that both speed and skill are impaired by excess tension. His argument for staying relaxed is now universally accepted by serious karate fighters. Not only is a relaxed fighter faster than a tense fighter but the relaxed fighter saves energy.

According to Lee, relaxation was a direct result of controlling the emotions. But Lee did not recommend relaxation to the point of lethargy. And he never advised training or fighting in a sleepy or unfocused mental state. He advised students to relax their muscles but not their thinking.

The energy you save by applying the 18 Principles to your techniques and to your strategies will go a long way for you in the ring. By staying relaxed you will last longer, move faster, hit harder, and win more.

Strategies for Mobility and Footwork

When I wish to avoid battle I may defend myself simply by drawing a line on the ground; the enemy will be unable to attack me because I divert him from going where he wishes.
                                                    —Sun Tzu, *The Art of War*

Assume a wide karate posture and plant both of your feet flat on the floor. Do you feel mobile or do you feel like you are stuck on high center and could not move fast enough to dodge a slow-pitch softball? Crazy as it seems this is the way many of your competitors will stand. From such a fully rooted and flat-footed position their slightest movement is a dead giveaway and an invitation for you to provide them with disaster.

When you shorten your stance and rise slightly up onto the balls of your feet, you gain kinetic mobility. Now as you move about keep your stance narrow and stay in balance. In this state it is extremely difficult for your opponent to determine what you are about to do. His ability to react to your attack is about one tenth of what it would be if you fought him from a deep static posture such as the one described above.

Your karate step is much like a boxer's shuffle step. I call it a two-step, and it is formed by standing with one leg forward and the other leg back. For example, try placing your left leg forward. Now push off with the right leg to gain distance. Your stance stays intact because your back leg (right leg) follows immediately.

The posture remains intact throughout any variety of directions or patterns of movement that you choose to perform. Practice moving forward and from side to side. Reverse the motion and retreat by pushing backward with your left leg and stepping down on your right. Be sure to bring your left leg back into position as you retreat.

Changing lead sides is a potent footwork strategy. It confuses your opponent and increases your range of techniques. Change lead sides only when you jump or move backward, never when your weight is on your front leg.

Another way to fool an opponent is by creeping up on him and punching him before he realizes that you have bridged his critical-distance line. Creeping is a footwork strategy that employs body fakes, shoulder jerks, and other deceptions designed to take your opponent's eyes away from your feet. While his attention is on your fake, your toes creep forward inch by inch.

Creeping can easily gain you an extra six inches against the distance you need to cover to close the gap. When you have gone the necessary distance, let loose with your technique. Surprise him with a little hyperextension and you have him.

Bruce Lee believed that the essence of fighting is in how you move. Develop footwork that allows you to move freely to either side and in all directions along vertical, horizontal, and curved angles. The basic step used by karate champions is very close to the box step, or two-step, used by boxers.

Learn the step patterns on both sides. Switch steps and change directions to confuse your opponent.

Mobilize yourself by shuffling, hopping, and creeping. Keep your knees bent but do not rest by falling into a flat-footed stance.

Be sensitive to the surface that you are standing on. Attempt to "feel" the floor with the balls of your feet as you move.

Do not try to use wide stances and long steps in a karate match. Tight footwork makes you mobile and makes your techniques hard to read. Footwork is your tool for changing your timing and rhythm.

Great mobility gives you unpredictability as a fighter. When the smoke clears and you carry your trophy out the door, your opponents will stand around and scratch their heads. They will be wondering how you did it, and they will never realize that it was your footwork and the resulting mobility that made you impossible to read and impossible to beat.

Your beaten opponent will go home thinking, "Boy, my timing was sure off today." He will never realize that it was you who threw him off by stepping fluidly around his stagnant postures and stilted patterns.

Almost all karate fighters are prisoners of their habits. Through all the years of his career the average fighter will keep the same timing. The chances are good that he will never understand the need to vary the rhythm and timing of his defense and offense. His blindness puts you in prime position for victory. Your footwork will teach a lesson that few will ever learn.

Strategies of Reach

Go into emptiness, strike voids, bypass what he defends, hit him where he does not expect you.
>   —Sun Tzu, *The Art of War*

When he began his tournament career, my student Thurman Karan had solid karate basics. His roundkicks were high and beautiful and

Turner uses hyperextension to reach her opponent.

his punches had power. His only problem was that he could never seem to hit anybody with them.

After months of frustration he hit a breakthrough point and suddenly began to understand the concepts of extension, hyperextension, and double hyperextension. He worked hard to apply these to his roundhouse kicks.

The next time he fought he reverted to his old short-range methods. Then suddenly he slid forward and at the same instant threw his roundhouse kick. The kick landed with a hearty thump. Thurman's face lit up with a brilliant smile and I knew he had it; he had an understanding of the basic strategy of reach, at least as it applied to the roundhouse kick.

Following that event I showed Thurman how to get the most reach out of all of his techniques including his sidekick, backfist, and reverse punch. Now Thurman covers huge distances with his lunging roundhouse kicks and other techniques. Nowadays he always surprises his opponents.

Strategies Using Centerline

One defends when his strength is inadequate; he attacks when it is abundant.

—Sun Tzu, *The Art of War*

You are a point karate fighter, not a kickboxer. You do not have to try to knock your opponent out. All you need to do is get the point. Full-contact fighters try to hurt their opponents and to do so they must land a large number of blows with rear arms and rear legs. Consequently they must face each other more frequently than point karate fighters who rely primarily on lead hand and leg techniques to gain their points. To throw rear arm and leg techniques they must expose their centerline and open themselves to counterattacks. Why should you take this risk?

Since you do not have to face your opponent very often, you can eliminate much of his offense by maintaining a defense that covers your center. There are many good defensive positions to choose from. Just make sure that the method you select covers your vital areas.

Most of the legal targets are along the center of your body, so it is necessary to turn at angles that protect your center and minimize your chances of getting hit. Keep your arms forward to give your centerline defense shock absorption. Holding your arms too close to your body

Turner uses her left arm to protect her centerline.

will deflect most blows, but you will still have to absorb most of the shock.

I used a high/low block to cover my center. I kept one hand up and one down to ward off all strikes to my centerline. My elbows were close together and my arms formed one straight line from the middle of my face to my groin. My lead hand was high so that I could throw my backfist. I could get into this centerline defensive position almost instantly.

Strategies Using Straight Lines

The momentum of one skilled in war is overwhelming, and his attack precisely regulated.
—Sun Tzu, *The Art of War*

The most direct way to hit your opponent is to strike him with your closest weapon and send your attack down a straight line. A straight line is the shortest path between your fist and your rival's nose. It is also the short road to tournament victory.

Straight-line attacks are extremely powerful and very hard to deflect. They provide the greatest economy of movement and they are hard to see coming.

Straight-line attacks have a tendency to cause an opponent to back up. The moment he retreats he is doomed. Follow with more straight-line attacks and you will eat him alive.

I deviated from this kind of straight-line assault only when my opponent was considerably more powerful than I was. When this happened I resorted to curved-line attacks that gave me a defensive edge.

Strategies for Faking

All warfare is based on deception. Therefore, when capable, feign incapacity; when active, inactivity.
                                    —Sun Tzu, *The Art of War*

In its simplest terms a fake is anything you do that makes your opponent think that something is happening other than what is actually happening. Your fakes offset your opponent's timing and earn you the advantages of distance and timing. Faking is the one principle that you cannot live without.

Delivering a fake is like telling a joke, but if your opponent does not react the way you want him to you are the one who misses the punch line. You must make him believe in your fake. If he does not respond you might as well get off the stage.

But how do you make your fakes believable? How do you get the maximum reaction from your opponent without overcommitting your fake and losing your ability to follow up? First your fake cannot look like a fake. Above all it must look like a real technique. Practice each fake until it looks exactly like the beginning of the real technique.

Even with his extraordinary speed, Bill Wallace found it advantageous to use fakes. He began using them early in his career. "I remember that people kept telling me I had really fast kicks with my front leg, but my opponents would block them," he said. "I kept wondering why, if I was so fast, people were able to block my kicks so easily. I realized that it was because they could see them coming. I reasoned that I could create an opening by drawing their hands to one area to block an incoming kick. I began throwing kicks to the stomach in hopes that they would see it coming and block and lower their hands. After a couple of shots to the stomach I would fake another midsection kick and then throw the third kick to the head."

Wallace recommended that every fighter incorporate fakes into his battle plan. "Most people fight by a method called throwing and hoping," he said. "They look for an opening, and then they attack it. When I fight I try to create openings. I thought if Mohammed Ali and other boxers can do it with their hands then I can do it with my legs."

Timing is the most important aspect of your fake. It does no good to make your opponent think you are going to throw a technique if he knows it cannot possibly reach him. The timing and the duration of the movement both play a major part in the presentation of a realistic fake.

You will have to practice each fake religiously in order to make it work. Strive to make each faking technique so realistic that your opponent will be unable to determine that your fake is a fake no matter how many times he sees it.

Once you perfect the mechanics of your fake you must learn to wait for the proper reaction. If you strike too soon, before he has reacted to your fake, you will negate the effect of your fake. You must learn to time not only your fake but your follow-up to the fake as well.

Jim Butin was a superb faker. "I used fakes to draw a picture for my opponent," he said. "I would throw several slow roundkicks that my opponent could easily block. After a few times he would get over his fear of that technique. He had become used to seeing that particular kick at that angle and was confident of his ability to block it.

"When I was convinced that he had a perfect visual image of the direction and speed of that technique from start to finish, then I would score by changing the angle of the strike or changing the technique right in the middle of the attack."

To better understand faking, try this little test. With your sparring partner throw the same technique at him again and again. Do it exactly the same way each time. When you perceive that he has "found" your timing on this technique, go ahead and try your fake. Fake the same technique and watch his reaction. You will notice right away that your opponent is timing you.

Make this timing drill a regular part of your training. By this method you can teach yourself the timing and broken rhythm necessary for effective faking.

Joe Lewis said faking leads to the ultimate goal of combat, which he described as "hitting your opponent without being hit." Faking is one of the most effective tools you have. Unfortunately very few fighters use fakes these days. Only a handful of coaches and instructors are currently teaching the fake. This is a shame, because faking is indispensable to a champion fighter.

Faking is taught in most other competitive sports. It is a regular lesson for boxers, football players, basketball players, and even racquetball players. Do not wait for our sport to catch up. Start teaching yourself to fake today.

Strategies Using Constant Forward Pressure

Keep him under a strain and wear him down.
                              —Sun Tzu, *The Art of War*

Jeff Smith was a tough fighter. He was a solid champion and a member of the United States Karate Team on our European tour. Fellow teammate Jim Butin remembers Smith's style well. Butin fought Smith five times, losing against Smith twice and winning three times.

"He was very versatile with a style similar to that of Chuck Norris," Butin said. "Like Norris, Smith used lots of good combinations. He did not have Lewis's blinding speed or tech speed like Wallace, but he was a bruiser. No matter what, he kept coming at you."

Smith was a winner because he had good technique. He was technically smart and he had a winner's attitude. He kept the forward pressure constant.

The theory of constant forward pressure is a defensive as well as an offensive principle. Most legal targets are found along the body's centerline, and most of your ability to attack is along a forward line. Keep forward pressure by maintaining a steady defensive position as well as a constant offensive drive.

Strategies of Timing

I make the enemy see my strengths as weakness and my weaknesses as strengths while I cause his strengths to become weakness and discover where he is not strong.
                              —Sun Tzu, *The Art of War*

Why should a sidekick thrown by Bill Wallace have a different speed, direction, and deceptive quality from the same technique thrown by a different fighter? Because of timing, individual techniques are as different as the individuals who use them. Timing is the essence of a fighter's style. Jim Butin gave me an excellent example.

"I beat a guy from Waco, Texas, by using a front-leg sweep. The next time we met in a competition he warned me that he had perfected his counter for my front-leg sweep. His exact words were, 'I have been working on that front-leg sweep. I have got your number, buddy. You try that on me again and it is all over.'"

"I fought him without using sweeps until I was several points ahead. Then just for sport I decided to try my sweep anyway. I swept that guy to the floor and hit him with follow-up body punches three times in a row. There was nothing he could do about it."

The point here is that Butin's opponent had been training against a front-leg sweep but he had not been training against Butin's front-leg sweep. "His training partner was not me. They were not applying the sweep with my timing and intensity," Butin added. From that experience Butin learned, and so did his opponent, that defense is not just a matter of defense against a movement. It is defense against the timing of a movement.

Bill Wallace's roundkick was not significantly different from anyone else's, but because of his speed and timing he was unstoppable. With the right timing, distancing, planning, and deception, you too can stick your foot into an opponent's face.

Strategies Using Angles of Attack

He who knows the art of the direct and the indirect approach will be victorious. Such is the art of maneuvering.
—Sun Tzu, *The Art of War*

I used straight lines to get most of my points. I deviated from this philosophy only when my opponent was much quicker or a lot more powerful than I was. When this happened I changed the line of my attack to incorporate curves.

If you have trouble getting in on a strong opponent, change your line of attack. Choose another angle and come in strong.

You can use the direct line of attack even in a defensive situation. Head straight into your opponent and defend or attack as necessary.

You can escape an attack by moving backward in a straight line, but you should never retreat more than one step. After falling back push into him again, making the straight line work to your advantage. Try to catch him between techniques.

Even with my training partners I got a shocked reaction when I changed my angle of attack from direct to angular. It confuses your opponent when you change angles. It is something new that forces him to pause, and that is when you strike.

When you change angles you break your established rhythm. Breaking your rhythm forces him to break his. At this moment he is weakened by the confusion of trying to figure out what you are doing. At this instant you will strike.

Assuming you initiated the attack, you can strike on this new angle before he can recover. Even if he is lightning fast the indirect attack serves as your equalizer.

Strategies Using Broken Rhythm

Offer the enemy a bait to lure him; feign disorder and strike him.
—Sun Tzu, *The Art of War*

This is the theory of broken rhythm in application. You can sucker the charger and make him run into your trap. When he comes in the first time, for example, let him chase you backward. Keep running away until you cross over the line. Act beaten as the referee gives you a warning.

Now he thinks you are a runner. He has an idea of what you will do when he next attacks. Unfortunately for him his idea is your idea. When he attacks again take a half step back and use your sidekick. Pow! Your kick will land. You got this point by breaking your rhythm and confusing his.

Joe Lewis seldom kicked above the waist. He used his backfist and his blasting sidekick with tremendous effectiveness. Jim Butin said: "His variety was in his timing, his broken rhythm, faking, deception, and especially intimidation."

The theory of broken rhythm also works with the initial move. You can fake your opponent by running backward or to the side. Then replant and push into him.

Jim Butin said: "I was a deceptive fighter. I had to be because I did not have the explosive speed of Bruce Lee or Joe Lewis. I did not have the combinations of Chuck Norris. My greatest attribute was speed. I had some speed with certain techniques—I managed to kick Bill

Wallace in the face once. Believe me, he does not get hit in the face very often.

"I once hit Joe Lewis in the face with a heelkick. He told me that no one from the D.C. club could kick him in the face, yet I did it. I don't believe I was faster than those guys. It was because I was sneaky."

Butin used broken rhythm aggressively to confuse his opponents and set them up for the kill. "I often did an offensive or defensive sidekick to the body with just enough force to make the guy hug his ribs. I would make it a crummy kick, sloppy and without much power. Sometimes I would just push him away to make him think I was slow, to make him think he could grab me and punch me the next time I tried to sidekick him."

Once his opponent's rhythm was broken, Butin was able to complete his strategy. He continued: "The next time, I would make it look like I was going to throw a light sidekick, but instead I would throw a fast heelkick to his face. Nine out of ten times I had the speed and accuracy to hit the guys right between the eyes with it."

Today's Fighters

Sadly, today's fighters seem to use less, rather than more, strategy. Too often the contests are won by the fighter who is simply the strongest. Strategy has given way to the less noble forces of brute strength and natural speed. More and more fighters are charging into each other, banging arms and legs until someone takes a hit.

The downside of this reality is that the art and quality of point karate may be slipping. One advantage is, however, that armed with the 18 Principles of Winning and the almost limitless numbers of strategies that may be derived from them, you can quickly advance to the top.

Turner in one of her trademark moves, a downward spiraling body wrap.

6
Competition Kata

Akata is a choreographed sequence of martial arts techniques. Traditional kata functions in four major ways. It is an easy way to pass martial arts techniques down from generation to generation. It is a tool for preserving a particular methodology of movement. It is a form of exercise. It is a type of moving meditation.

The Kata Controversy

For 20 years the martial arts community has argued about the value of kata. Out of this long debate three groups have emerged in kata: those who hold to the traditional view that karate kata should remain unchanged for the lifetime of the system; those who oppose kata; and those who modernize kata.

The traditionalists say kata is the backbone of a martial art. They insist that if you do not know kata you do not know karate. According to the traditionalists, kata is the foundation of both the physical and the mental/spiritual side of karate. Strict traditionalists believe that the creations of ancient inventors should be passed down from generation to generation with no change.

Bill Wallace had little use for kata. Like most top competitors he preferred to specialize only in fighting. "I didn't watch forms that much," he admitted. "I was into fighting."

A majority of those who fight in tournaments do not participate in forms competition, or if they do they do not take it seriously. Many argue that kata is a waste of time and that it has no resemblance to combat. They insist that movements invented centuries ago lack realism.

While the strict kata traditionalists argued with the hard-line anti-kata factions, the third group prospered in the tournament circuit. Those who elected to modify the traditional kata for competition or to create new karate forms especially designed for competition found the middle ground that set the standards for modern karate kata contests.

The Sacred Kata vs. Karate Art

Many traditional martial artists hold the ancient kata of their systems to be sacred. They consider the kata to be a living icon of the rich historical tradition of their style. Some practitioners even go so far as to hold their traditional sets as holy.

Personally I do not believe in the sanctity of the martial arts kata. I do not think that the creators of the great forms intended for future generations to attempt to perform their sets exactly as they did themselves.

Great teachers pass down the mechanics and the basics of their systems with careful regard to the principles and concepts that make each technique work. Great teachers do not want to spawn clones of themselves. These masters are people who found themselves through martial arts. They understood that to be as great as you can be, you must evolve beyond the mechanical and begin to express the martial arts in your own special way.

Van Gogh was a great painter, and many art students have emulated him. Baryshnikov is a great ballet dancer, and students study his movements. But the success of any artist is measured by the uniqueness of his art rather than by the similarity between his art and that of another. You might do the same steps as Baryshnikov, but you will be little more than a second-rate clone unless you find your own creative spark and express it within the art.

Like painting, music, and ballet, karate becomes art only when we transcend the traditional and mechanical movements that make up its core. Perhaps it is at the time when we begin to express karate as an art form unique to ourselves that our kata becomes truly sacred.

Traditional Form Secrets

As you have seen, I am not a traditionalist by nature. I built my kata career on mobile and creative expressions of the art and borrowed from many different styles to do it. This is the easiest way to become a champion, but I will admit it is not the only way.

You can succeed as a performer of strictly traditional kata if you do it with style. At one time I was certain that it was not possible to build a championship kata record with traditional sets. Two topflight traditional competitors proved me wrong.

Steve Fisher did not believe in flashy techniques. He did only traditional forms and traditional movements. He was the exception to a rapidly modernizing karate scene, yet he surged quickly to the top of his class anyway.

Fisher won with his traditional sets because he performed them with absolute precision. Everything he did was clean, crisp, and exciting. The focus of his punches was perfectly straight from the shoulder. His kicks were absolutely precise. His power was terrific, and his facial expressions were excellent.

Fisher had one secret that enhanced his performance. He embellished the timing of his traditional sets. I remember that he would count out his rhythm patterns like this: "One-two-three, slow, one-two, one-two-three." When he taught others he used this same method and clapped his hands to help his students learn his timing.

Marian Corcoran was another exception to the rule. She, too, won with strictly traditional forms in the heated and changing environment of kata competition. Her excellent traditional forms were powerful and precise. Her kata was like a poem in motion. Her rhythm varied in a manner quite similar to that of champion traditional forms competitor Steve Fisher. Marian Corcoran's secret? She was trained by Steve Fisher.

There you have it. You can succeed with strictly traditional kata if you have tremendous precision and if you are willing to vary the rhythm of your sets to add drama. I wish I could say that your chances of becoming a big-league champion with strictly traditional form is good, but it is not. Your chances are much better if you are willing to join the ranks of nontraditional competitors.

If you are a borderline traditionalist and you are not sure what to do, why not do it both ways? Keep the traditional kata sharp and formal and create your competition sets after the fashion of the modern creative talent you will be going up against. Keep the two separate. Why not be a traditionalist at home and a creative genius on the road?

Traditional Kata and the Creative Spirit

My instructor, Al Dacascos, taught traditional martial arts. We learned traditional sets, and our rank tests were based on our ability to perform the kata in its original pattern. For competition, however, Dacascos required his students to design their own kata.

The first time I was faced with the challenge of creating a competition form I felt that it would be impossible for me to do it. Developing an all-new form is difficult, and Dacascos's insistence on perfection made it harder. Finally my creative ability found its way to the surface, and I began to think for myself.

My designs combined traditional and nontraditional movements and emphasized martial realism. The freedom to create opened the doorway to self-expression, and soon I became the karate forms champion I had dreamed of being.

Dacascos was an advocate of creativity. He believed that the process of self-expression is necessary to the development of the martial artist, but Dacascos never abandoned the traditional aspect of the martial arts. His philosophy was to merge traditional techniques with nontraditional motions.

I can never thank Al Dacascos enough for instilling in me this liberated view of karate. He gave me the freedom to grow as a competitor, and this catapulted me to champion status.

To this day countless karate instructors doom their students to tournament stagnation by insisting that they attempt to perform a kata like clones of the originator. In my view it is time for the karate world to let the creative spirit out of the traditional bag.

Learn from the Best

My main instructor, Al Dacascos, was one of the best competition kata trainers of his time. But good as he was, he was only one person and represented only one point of view. Realizing this, he encouraged me to study from as many different kata greats as possible.

Dacascos knew that exposure to many different styles and many different stylists would broaden my view of the art. He realized that the perspective of other trainers and champions of kata would round out my understanding of competition and of winning performances. It is a mark of his greatness as a trainer that he was never jealous of his students.

Find a trainer who is open-minded about learning. Avoid trainers who forbid their students to learn from other sources. Stay away from

Instructor Al Dacascos (center), shown here with students, including Karyn Turner (left), was one of the best kata trainers of all time.

teachers who claim to be the only source worth learning from.

Of course, you will want to learn the basics of your style thoroughly before you branch out. Even Bruce Lee concentrated on one style for many years before he broadened his understanding of the arts by cross-training and researching other systems.

Once you have gained a solid grasp of the basics and have established yourself as a competitor, go ahead and turn up the heat on your learning process. Solicit the help of as many kata champions and champion trainers as possible. Attend the seminars at each tournament and, as Bruce said, absorb what works for you.

By taking tips from the best forms competitors around, I gained a wider view of the arts, and I also gathered a repertoire of movements that complemented my body. The nice thing about the martial arts is that movements from different styles are compatible. Hard-style techniques will blend nicely with soft kung fu moves and vice versa.

The Right Style for You

I began my martial arts career in Korean tae kwon do and eventually made a move to Chinese kung fu. Over the years I studied many systems and borrowed from not a few. Whether you are a beginner or a veteran martial artist, it is important that you keep your options open. Here are a few of the martial arts styles that play well in open kata competition.

1. *Goju-ryu*. One of four of the most popular Japanese karate systems.
2. *Shotokan*. One of four major Japanese karate systems.
3. *Tae kwon do*. A hard-style Korean system.
4. *Wado-ryu*. Another of the four major Japanese karate styles.
5. *Wu shu*. A modern form of Chinese martial arts in which students practice a mixture of traditional and nontraditional maneuvers.
6. *Isshin-ryu*. An Okinawan karate style.
7. *Hapkido*. A Korean system noted for its extensive use of kicks. Hapkido has no traditional kata, but its techniques are well suited for creative competition kata construction.
8. *Shito-ryu*. This major karate system is said to have originated in Okinawa and found its way to Japan.
9. *Chinese kenpo*. A system made popular by Ed Parker. Kenpo is considered to be the first Chinese system taught publicly in the United States.
10. *Choy Li Fut*. A Chinese system with both northern and southern influences.
11. *Chinese animal systems*. Tiger, crane, snake, preying mantis—and a whole zooful of systems make up this wide category. These styles are complex methods of fighting with forms that are rich with elegant postures.

These represent just a few of the martial arts systems from which you can pick and choose. There are hundreds of styles out there, many with solid traditions in kata. While one system may suit you better than another, it is important to remember that there are no superior styles, only superior competitors. You can be a kata champion no matter which style or styles you choose.

The Male and Female Attributes of Kata Performance

I classified myself as a soft stylist but I studied many styles, including tae kwon do, goju-ryu, and Chinese kung fu. My competition forms

Learn to distinguish feminine lines from masculine lines.

were considered soft, but they were actually built out of techniques from hard and soft systems. I incorporated anything from anybody if it worked for me.

Most of my forms included more soft-style moves than hard-style moves because I thought them to be a better fit to my body. Men and women are not built the same; we move differently, and our bodies tend to favor different rhythms and lines. Many power moves looked ridiculous on me. Few women look sharp when they do an excess of extremely macho movements in a kata. Conversely, many soft-style movements appear powerless when performed by men.

Soft-style techniques often hit "female" lines, which look wrong when done by men. Check the ratings and you will notice that there are many more male hard stylists at the top of the rankings than there are male soft stylists.

Soft-style forms are not really soft. They hide a great deal of power—perhaps more power than the hard-style forms. Soft sets are longer, more complex, and at least as deadly as hard-style katas. Unfortunately many of the moves in these sets hit female lines. They tend to complement the female body.

Does that mean that if you are male you cannot win in an open competition with a soft-style form? No. Eric Lee, Al Dacascos, George Chung, and many others have built their fame with the soft kata. These fighters modified their soft style to include more masculine lines and perhaps a few recognized hard-style moves.

Another excellent example of a soft stylist who prevailed is Tayari Casel. Casel had recognizable power in a graceful and masculine presentation. He had flow and power and no one could deny it. He accentuated the power and expressed his movement in masculine lines.

If you are male you must use caution if you want to win with a soft-style kata. Use a mirror to spot feminine lines in your form and eliminate them. Unless a movement complements your body it should not be included when you do your set in competition.

The same rule holds for women who practice a hard-style kata. A great many moves from hard styles do not complement the female physique. If a move does not look good, take it out or revise it.

Always choose the movements that complement your sex, your body, and your look. If you cannot bring yourself to eliminate a movement, then you must revise it. There is not a movement in any style that cannot be revised to fit your body and your style.

Kata competition is 80 percent presentation and 20 percent combative effectiveness. How you look is far more important than the effectiveness of what you are doing. The most effective and deadly techniques in your style may be inappropriate for kata competition.

Creating Your Own Kata

Few competitors attempt to create a kata entirely from scratch. With thousands of techniques to choose from, why should they? Creating a new kata is largely a matter of arranging old techniques in a new and unique sequence.

Begin by examining your own repertoire of techniques. Select the movements that you like and that you look good doing. Experiment with these pet techniques and perfect them as you play. Make a list of these special movements, as you will be using them when you get ready to create.

Select a favorite form from your style and watch yourself do each movement in the mirror. Freeze every move and adjust the postures as needed. Correct your stances and keep an eye open for the masculine and feminine lines. Raise and lower your punches and kicks as necessary. Lower your stances without going too wide and without sacrificing your balance. Keep mental notes as you go.

Before you spend too much time perfecting every movement, go through and earmark any movements that you do not like. Tag those techniques that you cannot do well or those that you do not look good doing.

Now go back to your list of favorite techniques. Substitute these special maneuvers for those that you have marked for elimination in your traditional form.

Somewhere inside your kata you may wish to insert a trademark move. This could be a technique of your own design or a borrowed technique. It should be unique and very flashy. The point of it is to create a signature for your form, which will become a recurring movement. This move must be excellent in order to be worthy of its bit appearance in every one of your performances.

You have now created your first nontraditional competition kata. Practice until you are secure and then enter a tournament. From your score you will know how successful your efforts to create were. Ask your judges what you could do to improve and take notes.

If you do not win first place, go straight home and get out your drawing board. Modify your competition set with the recommendations from your judges in mind. After you compete again, go through the same process.

Always watch other competitors. If possible get a videotape copy of the competitions you attend and study the moves of the winner. Borrow techniques that you like and insert them into your kata. As a courtesy you may wish to ask permission to use the maneuver if it is unique.

It is amazing what you can learn by asking others. Most champions are eager to share what they know. You will find that the people who are great at karate are not selfish with their knowledge. Most are flattered to be asked for help. Champions take their art seriously, and they enjoy a little praise for what they have done.

An experienced coach can give you pointers as you need them. The instructor's job is to assist you. He is not there to stifle you or criticize your efforts. If he does, it is time to get a new coach.

A good coach can save you years of work. The one you select may or may not be your regular karate instructor. Many fine martial arts teachers have little or no tournament experience. Do not confuse good martial artists with good tournament coaches.

Do not ask guidance of someone who has never done kata in competition. Go to the competitors and former competitors that you admire the very most. If there are no experienced coaches in your area, you will have to get what help you can from other competitors who attend the tournaments.

Sensational Movements

You are better at some moves than you are at others. No doubt you have several really sensational techniques that you look good doing. You probably have an even larger number of sensational movements that do not look too hot when you try to do them.

The karate tournament is not the place to perform techniques that you cannot do well, but a time for shining with your very best movements. You will impress no one by messing up extremely difficult maneuvers. You will make points for yourself by doing simpler moves well.

In this respect kata competition is similar to fighting. You know that most of the great fighters use a relatively small number of techniques. Successful fighters enhance the effectiveness of their techniques by applying the 18 Principles of Winning. In forms competition you can make plain moves look extraordinary if you do them well and apply the principles.

Do not try that jumping reverse spinning heelkick if you cannot do it well. Work on it at home but do not make it part of your performance until it is as sensational for others to view as it is sensational for you to do.

How can you tell what moves look good and what moves look terrible? The best tool you have is a mirror. Mirrors do not lie. There is no mistaking the reality that you will see reflected in your mirror.

Videotape recorders are your alternative tool for checking techniques. Video is especially useful when you are trying to determine if a jumping or spinning movement looks good or bad. Do not trust your feelings or the opinions of others completely in the matter of technique analysis. Sometimes a movement that feels sensational looks amateurish.

If you are an advanced practitioner and you have a wide variety of sensational techniques mastered and ready for performance, you should select a relatively small number to insert into each kata. Use your really hard and extremely flashy moves sparingly to enhance the many basic techniques that make up the core of a winning kata.

Winning Sounds

Do not underestimate the value of sound in a kata performance. The *kiai*, or yell, is heard in many martial arts styles. It is especially common to hard systems, but you can use the kiai to enhance your performance no matter what style you favor.

The kiai has great spiritual meaning in traditional karate. It also has practical value for offense and defense. The loud battle cry of the Oriental martial artist has the effect of making the person who yells feel bolder while at the same time startling his opponent.

The kiai also causes the body to tighten up. Many fighters use the kiai to tighten the body in order to better absorb an incoming blow.

Every kiai is unique. Bruce Lee developed an inane high-pitched scream that he used in place of the more traditional low-register shout. To date no movie star has effectively duplicated it.

Apparently Lee's kiai was a stage sound only. His widow, Linda, says that when he worked out at home he made no yelling sounds at all. Many of the Chinese styles do not use the kiai. Lee was a wing chun stylist in the beginning and probably never used a kiai in his early training. Nevertheless Lee realized the power of sound and incorporated a unique kiai into his martial arts films.

Should you develop a highly unusual kiai? Unless you are trying to get into the movies there is little reason to go to this extreme. All you need to do is shout. If your particular style has a special word or type of sound, go ahead and use it. The individuality of your kiai will come from the individuality of your voice.

How many times should you shout during your kata demonstration? I have heard performers shout as many as forty times in one set. The full dramatic effect of their kiai was fully lost by this overuse.

Your kata will last about 1 minute and 15 seconds. Three kiais are the maximum that you should use in one set of this length. Some of my weapons katas lasted 1 minute and 30 seconds. If you like long sets you might throw an extra kiai in, but for me two kiais were normal. Three get a little extra attention; any more sound stupid and bore the audience and the judges.

Elongating Movements

When you fight you want short postures and tight stance work. In forms competition you need exaggeration. You will not ever step into

Elongate the movements in your kata.

a full horse stance and punch in a fight, but you must do it in your form.

Think of the view that your audience has when you do your set. They are sitting far away, trying to see your karate in its most formal state. This is show time. Everything must be exaggerated and elongated if you want to be seen.

On the street you are going to kick with the ball of your foot, but in kata you will point your toe to stretch the movement. A roundhouse kick to the gut with the ball of the foot hurts more, but it looks dumpy under the lights.

Kata champion George Chung realizes the value of elongating his techniques. He does rapid multiple kicks and stretches each technique. For effect he sometimes shortens the last kick, emphasizing the strike by flexing his foot in order to hit with the ball of his foot or by blading his foot sharply in the case of a sidekick. He does this to show his judges that he is perfectly capable of performing the technique in the less showy but more traditional method of the old masters.

Perhaps you are a student of an art that has lots of entrapment movements. Such techniques are typically built of small circles and motions. Throws, grapples, and arm-trapping motions are not attractive in their realistic and combative form. Stand in front of a mirror and elongate each of these movements to find their hidden beauty. By stretching your movements you also make it possible for the judges to see what you are doing. No matter what style you practice you will get higher scores and more applause if you elongate your techniques.

Rhythm

If you stand before the judges and do your kata just as fast as you can and with each move perfect, will you win first place? Without rhythm you will be lucky to be noticed at all. Rhythm is the heartbeat of kata and without it your form will be dead on arrival.

By changing the rhythm and tempo of your set you give your kata drama. Hard moves mixed with fast, tense, and slow movements make a wonderful show. Even the most complex and well-executed techniques in the world will go without notice if they run together in a constant and bland speed. No move stands out in a kata that is performed without rhythmic depth.

Add rhythm to your kata immediately. Experiment with the following concepts and use music to create exciting rhythmic flow.

1. Add drama to your form by occasionally coming to a complete stop.
2. Slow down before you go fast to make your fastest moves look twice as fast.
3. Contrast three or four fast moves against three or four slower moves.

Splice in a wide variety of rhythmic variations to your set before you settle on the final form. If you have difficulty devising rhythmic patterns that make sense, you can use music to help you get a feel for the varied tempos of a winning kata.

Breathe!

A surprising number of competitors hold their breath as they perform their kata. Holding the breath depletes the oxygen in the body and causes the body to become very tense. Tension is not power, and too much tension makes even the hardest of hard-style sets look too stiff.

Holding the breath also deprives the body of energy, and the competitor who does this cannot jump high or perform the more difficult movements. The person who holds his breath during a kata demonstration will naturally gasp for air when the form finally comes to an end. Panting or heaving for breath makes the competitor look out of shape.

If you have a hard time making yourself breathe when you do your form you should realize you are not alone. Solve this problem by catching your breath during the slow movements of your kata. Practice daily to get enough breaths in during the slow times to ensure that your body is never starved for oxygen.

Lines and Angles

There are differences in the angles and lines used by the various martial arts systems. These differences reflect the fighting methods indigenous to the system. In a kata competition it is necessary to alter the angles of your traditional techniques in order to achieve the lines and angles that best show off your body. As an example let us do an exercise designed to perfect the angle of your front stance and your reverse punch.

Put on a long-sleeved uniform. Stand in front of a mirror, assume your forward stance, and extend your reverse punch. Take a mental snapshot of yourself, paying special attention to the angles and lines that form your posture. Now adjust your posture to attain the best visual angle possible. Grab a five- or six-foot stick or pole and then get back in front of the mirror.

Put the straight stick aside and assume your forward stance again. Make your stance as low as possible without throwing your body out of balance or into a stressful curve.

Take a look at your back leg and make sure it is completely straight. Bend your forward leg until your thigh is horizontal and your shin vertical to the floor. Now extend your right reverse punch.

Odds are that your arm is now parallel to the floor. This is fine for traditional kata and good for power, but it does not create the best visual line. Improve the look of your punch by raising your arm slightly.

Now take the stick and push it into the right sleeve of your uniform. Keep the stick inside your sleeve and slowly push it down your arm and under your shirt until you reach your waistband. Slide the stick under your waistband and down your right pant leg until it touches your ankle.

With the long stick running from your ankle to your wrist, assume your deep forward stance (bow stance) and extend your right reverse punch. Congratulations! You have just found the perfect line for a kata competition forward stance reverse punch.

Look in the mirror and take another mental snapshot before you slowly remove the stick from the inside of your uniform. Put the pole aside and try the posture again, making sure that your back leg and your punching arm form a straight line from the floor to the point at which the punch is fully extended. In my view this is the best punch that there is for kata competition.

There are so many different martial arts styles that it is not possible to say that all bow stances must be performed just as the one I have described. You may be a student of a system that uses much higher postures and relies on little known stances. Regardless of the system you are using you must be conscious of the lines and angles that your body assumes. Above all you must be consistent in your postures and in your use of lines and angles.

Another way to find the right line for each technique that you perform is to follow your hand with your eyes. If you do this you cannot help but give your body and your movement a look of importance.

Footwork in Forms

Now that you know about lines and angles in your postures and techniques, you are ready to learn some fancy footwork to help you get into those neat postures. Your footwork provides you with the smooth mobility to transfer yourself from one perfectly aligned technique to another.

Proper footwork lets you position the angle of your form so that the judges get the best view of it. Without good footwork you might run across the floor and do the most spectacular technique in the world at an angle that makes it completely invisible to your judges. The spectators might see it and cheer, but the judges mark you down and out. In a kata competition it is the view of the judges that matters, and it is your footwork that provides them that view.

Footwork enables you to keep relaxed and provides the foundation for your rhythm and flow. If your techniques are the bricks that your form is built of, then your footwork is the mortar that bonds the bricks together and makes sure that they line up straight with their best side forward.

Developing Charisma

Eddie Murphy, Arsenio Hall, Johnny Carson, and Chevy Chase all have charisma. You need some of it, but you do not have to be a stand-up comic to win kata competitions. Charisma in the karate world is a matter of showing out rather than showing off.

Few champions of kata competition are shy in front of an audience, but most are not extroverted to an extreme. You will have all the charisma you need by simply doing what you look good doing.

Go back to your mirror and work hard to perfect each technique in your kata. Now add the facial expressions that will further enhance and dramatize your performance. Smile a bit in places and grimace in others. Build your facial expressions into your performance and over-learn each segment.

When it comes time for you to perform your kata in competition, you will have every detail down pat. Your performance will be filled with the charisma that comes naturally to those who have total confidence in what they are doing.

Your charisma will increase as you add self-expression to your kata. Self-expression will come to you naturally as you gain full mastery over your kata. With the power of creative self-expression comes the magic of enthusiasm.

Complexity of Technique

Few sports give competitors as much freedom as karate. You can vary the complexity of your routines to suit the occasion or to satisfy a personal whim. The more complexity you include in your kata the higher you are likely to score. Just make sure that you perform your difficult techniques flawlessly.

Add complexity to your kata in stages. Include a difficult new move or a series of hot moves to your form, and then test it in a regional event. If the tough new techniques feel as comfortable in competition as they do in the dojo, then you have the material in demonstrative trim.

Some complex sequences are so difficult to perform that you will never be 100 percent certain that you will not blow the techniques in competition. The risk of doing such maneuvers is high, but the potential rewards may be worth it.

Perhaps you have seen gymnasts who add extraordinarily difficult movements to their routine. They are taking a calculated risk. If they hit the tricks they will receive a high rating based on the complexity of their performance. If they miss they will likely lose the event regardless of how well they did the rest of the routine.

You may wish to play these odds and add an extremely difficult section to your form. If you decide to gamble with extreme complexity, I suggest that you limit yourself to techniques that you can perform perfectly at least 80 percent of the time.

Some competitors maintain a highly complex series of movements to be used only in emergencies. They do not perform this risky segment under ordinary circumstances but insert it into their regular form only in a tied contest or in an especially close event. The complex segment is designed to fit neatly into the regular kata at a moment's notice.

Stances

Your stances should be as deep as you can go, provided that you can step out of them without sacrificing balance. Look in the mirror to see how low you can go and should go. Keep your stances at the same level and move as if you had a book balanced on top of your head. This gives your kata a smooth, flowing line.

With jumping moves and sweeping moves you will change the height of your postures. When you complete the jumping or sweeping technique, return immediately to your regular low posture.

Your horse stance (feet parallel, weight even between your feet) should be square like a box. Do not "drop your rear" in the middle of this stance because it makes the posture look weak.

Your bow stance (forward, or front, stance) should be deep, with the back foot planted flat. Practice until you have depth in all of your stances, including your cat stance (weight on the back leg, no weight on the front leg). When you first try your kata with low postures, you will suffer from soreness in your legs. You will be rewarded for this pain by strong legs and solid postures.

Make your stances as deep as they can be without sacrificing balance when you step out of them.

Winning Expressions

I learned the value of facial expressions the hard way. Once when I was photographed for the front cover of a national martial arts magazine I wore what I thought was my best look. It was a serious, respectful kind of a frown.

I got the message when I unwrapped my complimentary copy. What I thought was my best martial arts face was terrible. I looked like a pained rabbit. Immediately I set out to find the expressions that looked good on my face.

The right expression is an intensely personal thing. For me the right look was a cocky smile, which I used at the conclusion of each kata performance. In the opinion of those who coached me this half smile made me look proud and in control.

Use your mirror to find the expressions that look best on your face. You can use videotape and snapshots to help in your search for that certain look, but only your mirror will tell you the complete truth.

When you find the right facial expression you will perceive an immediate difference. Good facial expressions work wonders with judges and crowds. Find it now and you will never have to change it for the duration of your career.

How to Learn and Remember a Kata

A karate kata generally lasts more than a minute and has many complex movements. A kata that consists of thirty to sixty movements can be very difficult to learn; once memorized the material may be hard to retain. The longer the set, the greater the likelihood of an unexpected memory gap that blows the whole sequence. Memory gaps are especially likely under the intense pressure of competition.

You can learn a long form very quickly if you tell yourself that you need to learn only one small section today. Do not worry about the many movements to come. Your unconscious will allow you to learn faster if you categorize the material in this manner. When you focus on a small piece of the big picture, you remove the dread that comes from tackling a large project.

Memorize your kata in segments. A segment should consist of five to seven moves. Master each segment as a separate entity. Number each segment and think of your form as a collection of short units rather than as a long sequence.

This was my method and it saved me on many occasions. When my mind went blank during a kata performance I never panicked. I did not worry about trying to find my place in the set. If I got lost I simply jumped ahead to the next section and took it from there.

The Easy Way to Add Variety

Many traditional stylists that I know keep a large number of forms in mind at all times. If called upon they could perform all of the sets from white to black belt and well beyond. Most traditional systems have at least twelve forms. Some practitioners try to keep dozens of forms in their active repertoire. That is a lot of material to keep polished.

Keeping up your traditional karate sets is important to your martial arts heritage. But keeping more than two competition forms alive at one time is not necessary.

Open competition kata is different from traditional kata. To win you will constantly modify and alter your competition kata. As I have explained, I maintained variable sections for my competition forms, which I interchanged to suit the situation.

A competition kata is a masterpiece of karate styling. This is especially true in the higher ranks and in open divisions. The higher you get the more you will find it necessary to combine the best elements of many different forms into your performance sets. To try to keep more than two forms in this high state of readiness would take a great deal of extra time and would serve no purpose. The more time you spend focused on the competition kata the better your chance of victory.

Since it is so hard to get even one form into competition readiness, why should you bother to maintain two competition sets at all times? If you get caught in a tie you may be asked to repeat your kata. Your number two kata is your tiebreaker. It is your ace in the competition hole.

Some competitors change forms as often as they can. They fear that their form will be recognized as they travel the circuit. This is simply not true. After witnessing dozens and dozens of forms, very few judges will remember the details of a kata they saw weeks or months before.

Many competitors change forms frequently because they get bored with doing the same set again and again. Variety is the spice of competition, but changing sets too frequently does not give the kata time to "season." New material is challenging to perform but it is also easier to mess up.

When I became bored with doing the same kata week after week, to keep myself stimulated I changed my competition sets quite often. I managed to avoid the risks that come with performing all new material by replacing the kata by sections rather than by starting over each time from scratch.

My typical form had five segments. I might take out sections one and two and keep three, four, and five. I never had to replace a whole form all at one time. Even though you change your form just a little, it will look like a whole new form to those who judge you.

The Best Dress

Karate is hard work. Fighting and forms take a toll on your clothes. Competitor and trainer Jeri Van Cook found a solution for the rumpled look.

"I'd sweat like crazy every time I got near a competition," he said. "So I always showed up at the arena with at least two uniforms. One was for kata and one was for fighting."

Judges are influenced by many subtle things, including the look of your uniform. If you show up for kata competition in wrinkled and unshapely garb, you can expect to lose points. Make sure your uniform is clean and well pressed. If that means bringing several uniforms to a competition, then do it.

Your uniform should be formfitting. If possible wear custom-made uniforms so that the fit is perfect. The starch in your uniform will make you sound more powerful than you really are. The snapping noise made by a crisp uniform responding to a fast technique has a profound effect on the audience and judges alike.

All of my uniforms were custom-made, and I am certain that dressing in the best possible attire made a difference in the way the judges viewed my performance. My uniforms were worth every dime and more. (More tips on dressing are found in Chapter 7.)

Anything extra that you wear that moves and sways is distracting—especially jewelry. Forget about how much your ring cost or the special sentimental value of your gold chain. Take them off. Jewelry offends judges and does damage to your cause.

Facing Your Judges

As you design your nontraditional kata take care to place your best movements in plain view of the judges. Make sure that your best stuff comes off when you are facing the judges or when you are moving sideways in front of them.

If you have low and beautiful stances, be sure to do some of them at an angle that gives the judges a clear side view.

If you design your form in front of a mirror, you will not have trouble. The mirror will show you exactly what your judges will see.

Learning from Other Disciplines

Do not tell anybody, but I got a lot of my ideas from watching dancers, gymnasts, and drill teams. I certainly did not take much from these other disciplines in the way of technique, but I borrowed their concepts of timing, lines, tempo, rhythm, and showmanship.

I watched dancers to learn about the lines of the body. There is a great similarity in many of the movements made by dancers and martial artists, and I found it easy to translate the dancer's concept of artistic line into my martial arts techniques.

By watching dancers I enhanced all of my lunging techniques and greatly improved my ground movements. I converted many dance ground moves into martial arts sweeps.

From flag-bearing drill teams I got ideas for precision with weapons in my team demonstrations. I converted some of the flag-team movements into karate staff techniques and performed them all over the country.

Open your mind to other disciplines and you will be amazed by what you see. Add power to the leg lift of a dancer and you have a perfect kick. Put force into a gymnast's leap and you have a karate technique that is uniquely your own.

Earlier I mentioned my trademark move. I did at least three leaping butterfly kicks, spinning 360 degrees with each and traveling in the same direction. I followed with a front sweep, a back sweep, and then I jumped back into the air for another butterfly kick. When I landed I kept spinning and wrapped my body round and round in a downward—corkscrew—spiral all the way to the floor.

My trademark move never failed to get applause. Until now no one ever knew that it was inspired by a dancer who did similar movements using dance technique.

A song-and-dance man who wore a top hat and danced with a cane gave me the idea for a trademark stick kata move. He held the cane horizontally and then suddenly threw it down flat on the hard floor. The cane bounced back neatly into his hand. It was very flashy and though it had no meaning as a martial arts movement I took it for a trademark anyway.

The noise made by my stick as it rebounded off of the floor got me lots of attention, safely and dramatically.

The New Wave

Many tournaments now have special open divisions in which competitors may use music and weapons and a two-man kata is allowed.

Sometimes the forms are created by the students or the instructors. Sometimes a traditional kata is done to music. The purpose of this division is to encourage creativity in performers and to inspire the audience, who might not otherwise be able to relate to karate.

Add Music to Your Form

It is a bit harder to blend exciting changes of tempo and rhythm to your techniques without the aid of music. Without sound to guide you, you must add the drama to your form by imagining the music. Does this sound impossible? Most karate demonstrators think so—they simply perform their routines with the same dull rhythm all the way through. Solo kata demonstrations done to a flat beat have no life. Group demonstrations choreographed without cadence or variety in rhythm lack drama and seldom excite an audience.

You can ignite your audience if you choreograph your performance with imagined music. Build your performance around the eight count and insert highs and lows into your movement. Add stalls and tempo variations to emphasize your form, and you will stand head and shoulders above the dull masses of flat, rhythmless performers.

Other Performance Elements

Bowing with Style

The bow you do before your kata performance is different from the

Turner prepares to do a Chinese salute. Take into consideration the traditions of your judges when you choose a bow.

bow you do before fighting. You have the option to bow with style and with a theatrical flair. Just make sure that you do your bow with respect to the traditions of your judges.

A few judges have a "thing" about bowing. You could call it a grudge against informality. Traditional styles dictate strict rules for bowing, and traditional judges take those rules very seriously. (See Chapter 7 for more information about rules for bowing.)

Salutes and bows vary from style to style. I used a Chinese salutation that is quite simple and also fairly universal in the tournament world. To do this bow, stand with one hand clenched into a fist. Cover your fist with your other hand and then bring your hands to chin level. Now press your hands forward, keeping your hand covered.

You must keep your fist covered with your hand. If you open the fist, many consider this to be a challenge. If you expose the knuckles of the fist, it may be taken as a challenge to fight and as a symbol of disrespect.

Introducing Your Kata

Keep your introduction simple, short, and factual. The judges do not want to know everything about you and consider long explanations a waste of their time. Other competitors hate them because they bite into their time. The audience does not like long introductory speeches because they want action, and they do not want the event to run late.

Simply state your name, your style, and the name of your kata. Explain any special instructions or requirements needed for your kata performance. Then bow and get on with the form.

Concluding Your Kata

It takes guts to perform in front of others. With each performance we must face three psychological obstacles: the fear of beginning, the terror of forgetting, and the natural desire to rush away from the audience upon completion.

What you do after you finish your set is at least as important as what you do before and during. Even if you rush to the line and rip off a beautiful and complex kata, you will blow it if you hurry off like a frightened mouse.

When you finish your set and do your final bow, assume a strong and erect stance that implies control.

Look at your judges and give them a slight smile that says you enjoyed performing for them and that you are sure you did well. Hold this position as you wait for your scores.

When the judges showed my scores I always responded with a crisp bow. Then I backed up and did a practiced type of drill-team turn and marched out of the ring. If I knew the judges I walked away in a proud, crisp stride. If I did not know them I was especially careful not to turn my back on them.

Each day as you work to perfect your performance kata, you should practice ending your form and walking away from the performance area in a truly professional manner.

What You Practice Is What You Will Do

Michael Jordan does not practice sloppy jump shots, Joe Montana does not lob passes during spring training, and Sam Donaldson does not use slang when he is off the air. These men know that what they do in practice is what they will do under the lights.

Look around and you will find plenty of forms competitors who practice sloppy technique in the dojo while insisting that they will "do it right" on competition day. This is a self-lie of the worst sort.

How you practice is how you will be under pressure. Your mind has a tendency to stall out under the extreme pressure of a karate competition. The right half of your brain will take over, and your body will remember and do only those things that it has overlearned.

Better that you practice your kata three times with power and precision than twenty-five times badly. Practice every aspect of your performance as if you were center stage at the most important contest of the season.

Practice everything correctly, including your salute, your yells, your facial expressions, your postures, and your timing. Be intense and powerful. As someone said, "Practice does not make perfect. Perfect practice makes perfect."

After You Compete

As your karate career gets rolling you will begin to make friends of other competitors and of the judges. Make it a priority to thank your judges after every competition. This speeds up the process of making friends and lets them know that you are a serious contender for high honors.

Ask their opinions regarding your performance in a respectful manner. Judges are often criticized and mistreated, so they will appreciate your respectful approaches.

Take time to say a word of praise to other competitors in your division. Good will goes a long way in advancing your karate career.

Weapons Kata

Choose Your Weapon

Bruce Lee was responsible for the popularity of the nunchaku. The nunchaku is two short sticks attached together by a short rope or chain. At the height of his popularity Lee used the nunchaku in several movies, and an almost cultlike following developed for this weapon. At the time I was getting into weapons, it seemed that everyone was demonstrating with the nunchaku—so I stayed as far away from it as possible. So many competitors were using the nunchaku that the crowd and the judges were bored before the next nunchaku-toting contestant got to the floor.

The first rule for picking your weapon is to pick something that is a bit unusual. At the very least you should stay away from weapons that are popular.

Second, you should pick a weapon that is suitable for your body in size and in function. If you are five feet tall you probably do not want to wield a long sword. If you are six feet, four inches, a sai might look like a butter knife in your hands. Pick a weapon that fits your physique as well as your ego.

You have a wide variety of weapons to choose from in open competition. Here are some, each with a brief description.

1. *Long staff.* This staff, used in many countries, comes in various lengths and dimensions. The most common length is about six feet, but longer or shorter staffs can be selected to suit your build.
2. *Long spear.* Indigenous to many countries and many cultures, spears come in many lengths and are often adorned with colorful tassels.
3. *Three-sectional staff.* A long staff, sliced apart at two points and then linked back together with rope or chain. This weapon is of Chinese origin.
4. *Samurai sword.* A long curved sword, sharp on one side,

from Japan. Hilts protect the handle, which is long enough to allow for a two-handed grip.

5. *Double-edged long sword.* Both edges of the blade of this long and straight weapon are sharp. The handle for the long sword is guarded by hilts.

6. *Chinese broad sword.* The Chinese version of the broad sword has a thick blade that is sharp on one side. It curves slightly and is considered to be primarily a slicing weapon.

7. *Sai.* This short swordlike weapon has two curved prongs that act as a hand guard as well as a sword catcher. The sai is considered an Okinawan weapon.

8. *Tonfa.* A short, thick piece of wood with a handle. It is thought to be derived from a tool used by Okinawan farmers or millers.

9. *Butterfly swords.* These short and fairly thick swords are used in pairs. The weapon has a curved hand guard that completely covers the fist. The blades are straight with a curved cutting edge. This weapon is of Chinese origin.

10. *Hooked swords.* Hooked swords, originally from China, are always used in pairs and sometimes are linked together by their curved tips. Hooked swords have half-moon hand guards, which are sharp. The sword blade is sharp on both sides, and the base of the weapon is sharp and pointed.

11. *Kama.* This weapon, a small sickle attached to the end of a short stick, also comes from Okinawan farm tradition. Often two kama are used at one time.

12. *Nunte.* The nunte is like a sai except that one of the arched prongs curves away from the hand and the other curves toward the hand.

13. *Nunchaku.* Originally used by Okinawan farmers to flail grain. The weapon is comprised of two sticks attached by a short chain or rope.

14. *Chain.* A whip made of metal. This Chinese weapon comes in various lengths and is made of a variety of materials.

15. *Quando.* The Chinese quando is a heavy weapon with a large curved blade attached to a staff. A heavy, pointed spearhead is connected to the other end as a means of balancing this implement.

16. *Kali sticks.* Kali sticks are two short sticks usually made of strong bamboo. Kali is an art of the Philippines.

Pick a weapon that fits you in size and in function. Turner often used Chinese double swords, which are shaped like broad swords but are lighter.

17. *Chinese double swords.* Two swords come out of one sheath. Chinese double swords are shaped like a broad sword but they are lighter.

The list of weapons could go on and on. The chances are good that many of these Oriental weapons will be suitable for your body or can be modified to become so. With so many to choose from, how do you know which one to pick? Select a weapon that you like and looks good with you in the mirror and you will do well with it.

Flash with Weapons

If you learn to use one weapon really well, you will find that most of the movements can be translated to work with other weapons. This

Turner performing with kali sticks, usually made of bamboo.

made it easy for me to look flashy with any weapon with little effort.

I did the same flash moves with double steel whips as I did with Chinese double swords and arnis sticks. I did double figure eights with chains, double swords, the staff, and even the three-sectional staff. I recommend flash moves, but learn the basics first and make sure that you use the weapons correctly.

Balance Traditional with Nontraditional

While many moves will transfer from one weapon to another, there are some very pronounced moves that are special to each individual weapon. It is important that you include some of these traditional techniques in your kata to show your judges that you are well versed in the particulars of that weapon.

Be Safe

Certain safety rules apply to all weapons. For example, do not turn the blade of your sword toward your wrist. Most of these rules are based on common sense and may seem too basic to bother with. Do not overlook these rules. Your judges will not.

Make sure that your weapons are safe. There is nothing more horrifying to an audience and to a judge than to have a fast-spinning weapon come flying apart in the middle of a performance. Even replicas are dangerous if misused, so be careful.

Dressing Your Weapon

Some weapons are more dressy than others. My favorites were the double Chinese swords and steel whip because they caught the light. Their glitter and shine added spectacle to my performance. The faster I spinned and moved the better my weapon looked.

I dressed some of my weapons up by attaching a bright piece of cloth around the bottom or the handle. The cloth looked sharp as it moved through the air and it made a great sound.

A colorful piece of cloth helps the audience and your judges determine the speed at which your weapon is moving. The flash of your blade on one end and the bright color on the other make a beautiful eye-catching combination.

Showmanship

When Traditionalists Shine

The argument that karate performances should be restricted to exact reproductions of traditional moves in traditional sequences done in a setting as near to traditional as possible is refuted by the amazing demonstrations performed by some of the world's staunchest traditional masters. The common interpretation of "traditional" may be somewhat off the mark if we take into account the remarkable and unorthodox demonstrations exhibited over the past two decades by native masters of the traditional Japanese, Okinawan, Chinese, and Korean arts.

Ironically, these traditional masters have provided us with some of the most unorthodox types of demonstrations. By examining their creativity we can improve our effectiveness as competitors in the increasingly competitive universe of modern kata competition.

Masters of Stage and Sword

Mas Oyama is perhaps the world's best known traditional karate master. Oyama understood the effect that sensationalism of technique and performance has on an audience. To gain attention for himself and his art, Oyama regularly demonstrated martial arts techniques that defied the rigid tradition of his art. He routinely performed feats that no one else could do. During his prime, for example, he battled over fifty bulls. Many of these fighting beasts he dehorned, using only his bare hands. Others he sent to the slaughterhouse with a single death-blow from his fist.

Should you take a bull into the ring and kill it with your bare hands? Certainly not, but the point is that Mas Oyama earned his reputation by applying a tad more showmanship than was naturally present in the traditional system he championed.

Yoshiaki Yamashita, a goju-ryu stylist and traditionalist in the extreme, gained fame and earned for himself the nickname Cat by performing unbelievably high leaps. He would jump up into the air and deliver three lightning-fast kicks before landing softly, as a cat does. He caught arrows out of the air, and he trapped the razor-sharp blades of samurai swords in the palms of his hands. Of course, there are few alive who dare to criticize the Cat for being unorthodox, yet I know of no traditional precedent for catching arrows and snatching swords in the goju-ryu style. Was his traditional art diminished by his bold display of showmanship?

Fumio Demura is a Japanese stylist and a traditionalist to the core. He is also one of my favorite martial artists and one of the best demonstrators I have ever seen. Each summer for many years he performed at the Japanese Village in California.

Demura thrilled audiences with his incredible displays of power and control. Blindfolded, he knocked apples out of a student's mouth with a nunchaku. He threw kicks with a speed that would have made Bill Wallace blink. Realizing that it was hard to see his fast kick, he would sometimes hold his leg in the fully extended kicking position with his foot hovering an inch or so from his target. The kick was frozen just long enough for his subject to realize he'd been taken.

Demura's uncanny ability to freeze each kick—and punch—just long enough for his audience to see them was a marvel of timing. His performances were stunning. Few if any of today's demonstrators and kata performers have Demura's ability to gauge how long it takes for an audience to react to what takes place in a karate techniques exchange.

Tadashi Yamashita was a tremendous demonstrator and a master showman who used unusual and dangerous weapons. He was best known for cutting a watermelon in half with a samurai sword as it rested on the stomach of a student or a member of the media. He performed this stunt blindfolded.

Hidy Ochiai gained the attention of his audiences by lying on a bed of nails with a concrete block resting on his chest. A student would smash the block with a sledge hammer, causing no apparent damage to Ochiai's body. Nowadays the feat is frequently bastardized. Demonstrators lie on beds of nails, but they make sure all of the nails are at the same height. Ochiai's nails were sharp and of uneven lengths.

Ochiai was so skilled that he used his sword to split grains of rice on the forehead of one of his students. He was actually raised in a martial arts temple, and his combative skills were born from real "death wars" (personal one-on-one combat to the death) fought between schools.

Every demonstration he performed was full of excitement; each kata was loaded with emotion. The huge scar that ran all the way across his body, just below his rib cage on one side to the same point on the other side, reminded everyone that Ochiai was an authentic warrior.

Traditional tae kwon do master Jhoone Rhee earned his fame by demonstrating his sensational jumping techniques. In the sixties and early seventies he was the greatest leaper in the karate world. He routinely jumped into the air and splintered boards held at seven feet above his head. For variety he destroyed blocks of concrete also held at that height.

Ochiai accompanied the American team during our 1976 tour of

Europe. There I learned that his terrible scar came from a wound he sustained during a battle in which he defended the honor of his school. As the school's best student, he was selected for the privilege of solo combat.

I saw Hidy Ochiai years after our karate tour of Europe in 1988 at the Battle of Atlanta. He recognized me right away, and it wasn't long before he gave me his opinion of the state of affairs of karate today. "There is no talent left in the art today," he said.

He seemed a bit upset by the competition that he was witnessing, but when he enrolled himself in the kata competition I was completely shocked. I do not know how old he was; suffice it to say that he was a very senior martial artist.

His form was filled with fire and emotion. His moves were alive and precise. He had the power and charisma of a much younger man. And he took first place in forms at the 1988 Battle of Atlanta. When I asked the senior master why he had entered himself in the competition he explained it this way: "I was so mad [at what I saw] that I entered kata today. I walked out there to show them what karate kata is like."

The point of these examples is that the traditional karate masters won their fame by performing outlandish and theatrical demonstrations of their martial arts ability. Not one of these ultratraditional masters is remembered or noted for his conservative performance of an ancient kata. If the most traditional masters of the karate establishment felt free to express their art creatively, why should you limit yourself?

Showmanship Techniques

A martial arts demonstration is no different from any other type of stage performance. The standards that govern a martial arts performance also govern dance and drama. The same rules for presenting yourself to the audience that apply to all expressionistic art forms apply to martial arts and kata demonstrations. This means that if you wish to build a name for yourself in kata you have to be more than a good martial artist—you must also be a showman. When you perform karate before an audience your job is to entertain as well as demonstrate techniques.

Karate expert Ed Parker was an excellent performer. He was nicknamed the Hollywood Karate Exhibitionist, and he continually lived up to the name. Parker had a flair for demonstrating, he possessed excellent karate skills, and he never failed to entertain with humor.

With showmanship Parker got the karate message through to hundreds of ordinary people. Ed Parker presented karate in a way that everyone could relate to.

My karate demonstration team was called The Hard Knocks. Some laughingly called us the Kiss karate team after the rock group Kiss because we performed with strobe lights, black lights, explosion boxes, and smoke machines.

Karate is a mystery in the minds of the public. The best karate showmanship employs mystery as a means of giving the viewers what they crave. You must incorporate showmanship into your karate performances and into your competition kata. When you add mystery to your performance you add life to your karate and drama to your demonstration.

Choreography

When I formed The Hard Knocks demonstration team I had had years of kata and karate demonstration experience. The group was immediately successful, and soon we were traveling and demonstrating all over the world.

Our engagements included performances at Las Vegas casinos, major showrooms, television specials, and virtually every karate tournament. We even performed for Princess Grace in the palace in Monaco.

Our success came not because of the ability of any one person but because we thrived on teamwork and avoided especially spectacular individual moves. Each segment of our performance was carefully choreographed to expose the full power and skill of the group.

Often we performed on very small stages. We did many shows inside boxing rings where space was limited, yet we never missed a move. The reason that we were able to act as a team with total unity was because the entire performance was choreographed to an eight-count beat.

I will admit it now; I stole the idea from dancers. Much as a choreographer would choreograph the movements of each dancer in the *Nutcracker* ballet, I choreographed to music the movements of swords, whips, ropes, kicks, punches, and other potent martial arts maneuvers. Yet none of our audiences ever seemed to associate our performances with dance. To this day people ask me how we managed such coordination of movement in such tiny areas.

To train The Hard Knocks team I would count one through eight

Karyn Turner's Hard Knocks karate demonstration team. The Hard Knocks performed all over the world.

and match each movement of each performer to that timing. No team member had to watch another team member to stay in synchronization. Because all members were counting to the same timing, all movements happened in perfect synchrony.

It was this precision of movement and the flow of the eight count that made our performances so popular. When the hard beats hit, out came the explosive movements, such as jumpkicks. When the tempo was slow, the team did tension moves; and when the music exploded again, so did we—right on the beat.

Choreographing the movements to an eight count—which worked better than any other method—rocketed The Hard Knocks to stardom. It also made my job of managing the group much easier. You might imagine that the hardest challenge of all would be replacing a member of the team with a novice performer, but this was not the case. Since everything was done to the eight count I was able to train a new member very quickly.

All of the performances by The Hard Knocks were done to music. When you demonstrate for your school or when you perform your kata in tournament competition, it is unlikely that you will have this advantage. Without the steady beat of the music you have no standard to attach your moves to. Without music you cannot choreograph to the highs and lows of the instruments and the changing rhythms of the song. Do not despair, however, because you can put the music into your demonstration without the song.

Winning Thoughts

Once a kata was simply a method of remembering. Kata preserved the techniques and the methodology of a system. Nowadays kata continues to do all of this but it does more. With the popularization of modern karate tournaments kata has also become a vehicle of self-expression for the progressive martial artist.

Competition kata is not a replacement for traditional kata; it is an enhancement. No longer are students afraid to create new movements and combine old and proven techniques into new arrangements. For the first time in the long history of karate it is acceptable for the average student to explore and expand on tradition.

7
Tournament Structure: How the Tournament Circuit Works

The point tournament circuit is a complicated maze that confuses the majority of all competitors. The procedure and structure of karate tournaments vary so much that even veteran competitors remain fuzzy on the rules, on the politics, and on the policies of tournament life.

To keep a clear head in this highly competitive world you must first determine what type of event and which events you need to participate in to gain points and national recognition. And in order to succeed in this exciting but confusing universe you must learn the inner workings of the major events themselves—the whos, the hows, and the whys of the important karate tournaments you will be attending.

Without a working knowledge of how the point tournament circuit works you could waste years fighting the wrong fights and performing the right kata at the wrong events. Since the traditional karate tournament circuit is a tricky pathway, with rule variations, differing point values, tournament ratings, and political pitfalls, here is a map of sorts to guide you—an examination of the different types of martial arts tournaments.

Types of Tournaments

Closed Tournaments

There are many types of martial arts tournaments. Some competitions are open to all comers and all styles. Others are closed to all but the members of the particular school or organization that is sponsoring the event.

Closed tournaments are common among several of the larger and better-established martial arts systems and the organizations that promote these systems. One good example of this practice is seen in the competitions produced by the American Tae Kwon Do Association. This association, which, by the way, is an excellent organization, regularly presents closed tournaments in which only their own members can compete.

Some closed tournaments are very large. A few of them are almost as large as the huge national karate tournaments.

If the martial arts group or organization that you belong to offers closed tournaments, you may wish to participate in them for fun and to gain experience. But closed tournaments are, well, closed. Nobody outside of the club will get to know about you. If you are serious about attaining national status, you must quickly graduate out of the closed variety of martial arts competitions and into the open tournament segment of the karate world.

Traditional Open Tournaments

Open tournaments are those tournaments designed for all styles to compete with and against each other. Only in open tournaments can you earn the rating points necessary to become a nationally recognized competitor and champion.

Open tournaments vary in content from city to city and event to event. Some of these tournaments have divisions separated by style. Often in an open tournament the kata divisions are arranged to match up competitors in the same styles. There may be divisions for soft styles that lump arts such as kung fu, kempo, and wu shu together, and another division for all hard styles, such as Korean arts and Japanese systems.

The event that makes the clearest distinctions between martial art styles is Ed Parker's renowned Internationals Tournament. At the Internationals, the divisions are separated not just by the general categories of hard and soft but by style within the larger categories. There is a division, for example, for tae kwon do, one for kung fu, one for Okinawan karate. A large number of the world's major martial art styles are represented by divisions at this grand karate event. Currently the Internationals is the only tournament that separates divisions according to exact style and not simply by the broad categories of hard and soft martial arts.

Fighting is another matter. Few tournaments have separate divisions for fighting.

Within the world of open tournaments there are a number of different types of events. There are local tournaments, regional competitions, and national events such as Ed Parker's Internationals, Joe Corley's Battle of Atlanta, and John Worley's Diamond Nationals. All of these tournaments, big and small, fall into the broad category of traditional karate.

By traditional I mean open karate tournaments. These are nationally sanctioned point tournaments. They should not be confused with full contact karate, or kickboxing, events.

Sport Karate Tournaments

Full-contact karate is the sport side of martial arts. Although American kickboxing is the "child" of traditional karate, none of the rules of traditional karate competition apply to the full contact sport.

It is easy to spot the difference in a point fight and a full contact sport match. The full-contact sport of kickboxing is much more highly organized than the traditional karate circuit. The promoters and organizers of full contact karate have uniformity of rules and consistency in judging, refereeing, and scoring. Unfortunately all of these organizational attributes are currently lacking in the universe of traditional karate.

The Variety in Structure and Personal Guidelines

Sport karate has evolved a system of self-government similar to that of a kingship, while in contrast traditional karate tournaments are governed almost entirely by the individual sponsor. At a traditional event the promoter makes the rules and decides who are to be the judges and referees. His authority is like that of the powerful warlords of ancient China and Japan. Each individual warlord ran his own castle by his own rules with the least amount of regard possible for outside powers.

With rules and regulations being decided on an event by event basis, naturally the rules vary widely from contest to contest. It is partly because of this variety in the structure of tournaments that the competitor must have personal guidelines. For me those guidelines have always been the 18 Principles of Winning listed in Chapter 1.

The principles work at all events regardless of the rules and conditions. They are designed to function universally by theory rather than by style or personal technique preference.

Do not despair about the variance between events because the 18 Principles of Winning apply to all tournaments. At least one theory of every principle applies to any type of situation in any division. Without the application of the principles it is virtually impossible to win consistently at major events.

Do not become confused by the many different types of competition events. By reading about events, going to events, and competing in events you will gradually be able to sort the grain from the chaff. Soon you will be spending your time, money, and energy on the right types of tournaments at the right times.

Sign Up

Now that you have identified what types of tournaments you will be competing in, you need to decide which tournaments to enter. Your instructor should be able to assist you. If your instructor is not familiar with national competition or competing in open tournaments, do not worry. Check newsstands for martial arts publications. Many of these monthly and bimonthly magazines provide a schedule of tournament events. Many list the promoters as well, and some include ads submitted by the promoters.

Whether your instructor is experienced within the open karate tournament circuit or not, you should spend some time calling around. Talk to promoters and sponsors of various events. Very quickly you will begin to make distinctions between the events that will be valuable to your career and those that will not.

Also in your favorite martial arts magazines you will find out who is who in the karate world you are about to enter. Associations that sponsor karate events list by rank all top competitors in all divisions according to points awarded when they win first, second, or third place.

You will find it a great help to buy the magazines and make lists of the events and their promoters. Then write to the promoters to ask that they add you to their mailing list. Request that they send you their rules, their yearly schedule, and registration for specific events. Do this to get started, and remember that after you enter a tournament you will be automatically added to their mailing list.

There is almost always a fee, paid by the competitor, for each division in a tournament. If you enter fighting, form, and weapons, sometimes you will get a price break. For example, there might be one charge to enter a division, perhaps $25, and a smaller amount for each additional division you enter.

You can preregister or register at the door. Promoters, however, love to preregister competitors. It works to their advantage because they can begin bracketing the divisions in advance and waste less time on the day of the tournament. Since the promoter wants so badly to preregister as many tournament participants as possible, he or she usually offers a discount. A preregistration fee is almost always less than that at the door on the day of the event.

Levels of Competition

Each division in a tournament is divided into levels or divisions. Most promoters separate the competitors according to rank and age. There could be, for example, a division for fighting with levels for green belts ages 6-8, 9-11, 12-14, and so on. Larger events will generally have more categories for age and rank.

In the majority of events, you will be allowed to compete up in rank or age but never down. If you are ranked as an orange belt or a gold belt, for example, you would be allowed to compete in the green belt division but not in the white belt division.

To begin with, compete at the level of your current rank and age. Competition should be challenging but not overwhelming. If your fight feels like hell on a warm day you may not yet deserve the rank you carry. If you enter your own division and wipe out all comers with no sweat, you are probably ready for a higher level of competition— regardless of the color of your belt. Keep testing yourself until you find the level where you really belong.

During his college years, Bill Wallace proved how vast is the discrepancy in ability among fighters of the same rank. Unlike his university classmates who spent their vacations at the beach or on the slopes,

Wallace spent most of his driving across the country with top-ranked fighter Glen Keeney. Together the two visited as many karate schools as possible along the way.

"We would stop at different karate schools and spar everybody in the school. Everybody," he writes. Wallace would drive as far as he could and then return along a different route so that he could visit even more schools during the trip home. "We'd fight a white belt at one school who might be the equivalent of a brown belt at another school. . . . I have been nailed, and nailed good, by white belts and haven't been touched by black belts."

Wallace contends that the variance of ability continues today. "Sometimes at my seminars I'll pair a white belt and a black belt. If you ask them to take off their belts, a lot of the time you cannot tell which is which during a sparring match."

With such a broad range of ability being classed under the same rank levels, it may take you quite a while to discover exactly where you fit. And even after you determine what level of competition you need to be in, you should occasionally fight in the next higher division. This continually affirms your status, gives you experience, and acts as a monitor of your abilities.

Fighting in a tougher division in smaller local tournaments is good training for the major league competition you will be facing when you go national. In karate as in all sports we make the greatest advances in skill when we face a superior opponent. But when you become a serious contender for rank in the national events, stay in your own rank and age level—every point counts.

Competition on the national level means food and hotel bills and travel costs—it is an expensive way to learn. You will save lots of money if you take time to evaluate your rank and status before you make the jump into the national circuit. Spend enough time earning your stars in the smaller, less heated, events near home. You will know when you are ready for the big time.

Rating Points

If you intend to become a national competitor you must get a rating. Pack your bags because you will be doing your share of travel. You don't have to travel, however, to every single karate tournament that you can find. Just pick the specific tournaments that can render the national rating points you need to become a karate champion.

You do not have to attend more tournaments than your rivals; you simply have to attain more points than your rivals. Do this by winning more first, second, and third place competitions than they do. Make as many events as you must to get the points that you need.

By winning you accumulate points and by being seen again and again at major events you develop a reputation among the judges. Once you have established yourself as a winner in the eyes of the judges, you secure a powerful psychological advantage. A judge who remembers you as a winner will expect you to win again. That puts the odds in your favor.

Tournaments, like the fighters themselves, are rated. Tournaments are classified as either A, B, or C. If an event is rated C it means that points earned at this event will be valued at two-thirds of the rating points of a B-rated event and perhaps only one-third the value of points won in an A-rated event.

These ratings are assigned by the tournament associations. Several factors influence the rating process. For example, an event may be given a C or B rating because its promoter failed to submit the necessary registration materials or was negligent in any variety of areas.

A-rated tournaments are so classified partly because a substantial amount of award money is distributed at them. At an A-rated event there will be cash prizes for the top fighters. Dollar awards will go to the three or four top-scoring forms competitors and a certain amount will be given to the best weapons competitors.

At John Worley's Diamond Nationals Tournament winners are rewarded with diamond rings. These valuable rings are awarded in place of cash. Worley's Diamond Nationals, one of the top events in the country, is an A-rated tournament that draws top contenders from all points on the map.

In order to be officially recognized—that is, in order to be able to award points—tournament promoters must pay a sanctioning fee. The size and magnitude of the promoter's event (A, B, or C) determines the size of the fee. This money is the main determiner of the status of a tournament event.

Rating points are awarded per weight division and sometimes by geographical region. You can be rated in your region whether or not you compete for national points. Normally you will have regional ratings in addition to national ratings.

Karyn Turner with John Worley, the promoter of the Diamond Nationals Tournament, which draws top contenders.

Publicity

You need more than points to become a nationally known competitor—you need fame. To take the worst case, you could find that after years of winning tournaments you remain a virtual unknown in the wider karate community. The majority of martial artists will not even know that you are alive, much less that you are a winner. Even folks in your own hometown will shake their heads when asked if they know your name.

Without publicity you will find it very hard to gain the political support, the monetary support, and the recognition that a champion deserves. Publicity is as important to your success as the cash prizes you will earn and the trophies you will be placing on every horizontal surface in your home.

Opportunities for movies, advertising endorsements, books, and paid lectures are not offered to the unknown. Properly cultivated, your well-publicized reputation as a champion fighter gives you instant credibility in the lucrative seminar circuit and can make a world of difference in the success of your future karate school.

If you win enough you might eventually get some publicity. Unfortunately if you wait for the publicity to come to you it may come too late in your career to do you much good. Take matters into your own hands and become a champion of publicity at the same time you are becoming a champion of the ring.

Press Release

First you need to develop a press release. Do not wait until you win the big one to have your press release written. Get started on this as soon as you have something to tell. Plan on updating this invaluable tool frequently.

A press release is a résumé of your achievements. It should include a photograph, a brief personal-background biography, and an upbeat description of your accomplishments as a nationally rated karate competitor. It should be short, sharp, and professional in every detail.

Spend the time and the dimes to have this done right. Get a good photographer for the photograph. You are a fighter, not a writer, so hire a professional to write the text. Misspelled words and bad grammar in your biography will make you look like a loser no matter how much you win.

A professional print job is also a must. Ask the printer to produce plenty of copies as you will be distributing them liberally.

Use your press release to advance your cause with newspapers in your area or in the area where important tournaments are being held. Give your press releases to various groups or schools that may ask you to speak. Your press release should be submitted to promoters and sponsors of events in which you participate. And make sure the martial arts magazines get your press release, especially after any big win.

The promoter is responsible for getting your rating points into the rating system and into the various magazines that print these results. He has thirty days after each event to submit this information (the associations often publish the names of promoters who fail to do this).

You are responsible for sending photographs of yourself and any required biographical information to the organizations and publications that track the point ratings. Magazines need photographs, and promoters cannot possibly provide pictures of all of their champions and top contenders.

Getting your photograph and your press release into the hands of the editor after every major win makes the editor's job and the promoter's job easier. Do this consistently and you will find yourself getting the publicity you deserve, especially if you make sure that the pictures you send are sensational—black-and-white, with lots of action. The importance of magazine coverage to the career of a karate professional cannot be overstated.

Magazine Coverage

Magazine editors do not have the time or the money to chase karate champions across the globe. Nor do they have the resources to cover every karate event. As soon as you start winning begin to develop relationships with the magazines.

Decide on an angle that you believe would interest the readers of the karate magazines in which you want to gain coverage. Find a writer experienced in writing articles for martial arts or other sports-oriented magazines. Get approval from the editor and have the article written. Be sure to employ a writer who takes good black-and-white pictures, and remember it takes an average of six to eight months from the day you submit to see anything in print. Get busy!

Martial arts magazines need stories badly, but they are not likely to print a profile or biographical article on you no matter how much you win or how good you are. It is much easier to get publicity for yourself by teaching others what you know—how to win tournaments, for example. You can get plenty of coverage in print and in pictures if you take this approach.

Most people sit and wait for the magazines to come to them. Sometimes it never happens and a star-quality fighter remains a "champion without a face" for the duration of his career. Do not wait; find a writer and get your story told as soon as possible and as often as possible.

Who Are the Officials?

Judges

Usually there are no qualifications for judging other than a black belt status. Even a black belt who fights but never competes in form can judge form and vice versa. It seems to me that there is no method to the madness. The poor quality and almost nonexistent qualification requirements for judges in tournaments of all sizes and ratings is my biggest pet peeve about the point tournament circuit.

If a black belt comes early to an event and participates as a judge, he is allowed to compete himself for free. This is his incentive to judge, and the bias problem this creates is quite severe. This lack of professionalism on the part of promoters is unfair to competitors and detrimental to the entire institution of traditional karate.

As I have mentioned, rules vary from event to event. The promoter of a tournament holds a rules meeting for the black belts who will be judges before the tournament begins. Unfortunately, few judges are quick enough to pick up on the many rule variations specified for the event. Some black belt judges routinely ignore the rule modifications anyway and simply judge the way they want to judge.

At tournaments you find various combinations of judges and referees. There might be, for example, four judges and a referee, three judges and a referee, or two judges and a referee. It all depends on the promoter's preference.

It takes an extremely talented and positive individual to overcome the shortcomings of the judging system, but by understanding these idiosyncrasies you can always be one step ahead of the competition. Think of the judging problem as part of the challenge, part of your opportunity. Remember you are in competition to win, and to win you must play their game.

Cutting a Judge

In spite of the shortcomings of the judging system most judges have their hearts in the right place. There are exceptions, of course, and too frequently a really bad and totally unqualified or biased person is allowed to judge. Fortunately, as a competitor you are allowed to request a change of judge providing that you do it before your fighting or form division begins. It takes guts and it may seem like an impossibly bold move, but you must be prepared to demand (nicely) that a judge be dropped from judging your division if you feel that it is necessary.

I often requested removal of an official if I felt that the individual wasn't qualified to judge my form or fighting. I made my decision to exercise this right by watching the judges as they judged contests prior to competition in my division. Often I knew the person from previous tournaments and so was able to make an instant decision. Either way, if I believed that a judge was unqualified, I asked for a cut.

If you see a judge who makes wild calls or one who clearly has no opinion of his own and merely follows along with the majority, ask for a cut. It is likely that you will have to exercise this option frequently, and when you do you should expect that the individual you have rejected is not going to like it. But as long as you make your request respectfully and tastefully you have nothing to be ashamed of.

Do not misunderstand me. I am not in favor of whining and moaning about imagined prejudices and problems. Ask for removal of a judge only when you are certain that the individual is biased or unqualified. If you compete nationally you must take the responsibility to screen incompetents. Believe me, there is nothing more frustrating than spending a lot of money getting to a tournament only to be judged by someone who does not know what he is doing.

Unless you are familiar with the judges you must evaluate them at the event. If possible, observe the judges who are going to be assigned to your ring. If you cannot determine which judges you will be facing, then you should attempt to watch all of the judges in as many different areas as possible. The bad ones will stand out. If one of these comes into your ring, be bold—ask to have him removed.

Referees

Referees are selected in exactly the same manner as judges. If you have a black belt you can be a referee. Sometimes referees are paid but most often they are not.

It has been said that having a high school degree does not mean you are smart and having a black belt does not mean you can fight. This is true—and a black belt does not mean you can referee either. Currently there is no dependable way to determine whether an individual earned his black belt in the ring or whether he simply walked into a supply house and bought the thing. Whether a referee is good or not depends on his experience, his natural ability to observe action, and his ethics. You might say that there are two losers in every karate bout, the person who gets the least number of points and the referee. As it is with basketball and other sports, in karate the official is always criticized for doing his job. It is a tough and thankless task.

What Motivates the Officials?

Referees, like judges, do this no-win work for a wide range of reasons. Some do it for the experience. Others lend a hand because they want fair judging and feel that they are capable and therefore obligated to help. As it is for the judges, the main motivator for referees is the fact that they receive free entry and a competition-fee waiver. Occasionally there is the totally unethical person who asks to referee with the secret idea of swaying points in favor of his own students.

Some black belts referee to gain recognition and ego gratification. It can benefit their status as leaders and instructors to have their students and peers see them act in this official and important capacity. Often a black belt will offer his services as a judge or a referee in exchange for help in an upcoming event that he is sponsoring. By helping they gain good will. Some do it for the opportunity to provide brochures and other advertising for their own karate tournaments.

With such low standards for officials there tends to be a political influence in many tournament events. Although it is a standard rule in all events that no judge or referee may officiate if he has a student in the ring, it happens more often than not.

Sometimes this violation is accidental, and sometimes it is the result of personnel shortages. As a competitor, when this happens you have three choices: not to compete; to compete and then complain about everything that happens (which is what the majority of competitors do); or compete and rely on the 18 Principles of Winning, using them to overcome political and technical problems. With the principles you can consistently walk in and out as a winner. You do have the right to protest the outcome of a fight if you act immediately, but unless there has been an extremely clear violation of the rules, a protest will seldom gain the desired effect.

With few exceptions I have no pity for competitors who scream about losing a point. Contestants who cry over a loss in kata or fighting, all the while blaming their woes on judges and officials, are wasting their breath. The time to evaluate the strengths and weakness of a competition situation is before not after the battle. It is the fighter's responsibility to evaluate each situation and prepare an action plan before he enters the ring. Most people who lose and then complain are lazy. They fail to take the time and make the effort to adapt to the peculiarities of the situation. They lack the versatility of a champion.

You must watch the judges, the officials, and the competition. Let's face it: there are always, in everything you do in life, people you feel are not being fair. But the person who surges ahead is the one who makes the best of each situation. The champion is intelligent enough to take control of the environment and use the fighting principles to gain the best advantage possible with regard to biased judges, unusual rules, and a ton of similar "unfair" happenings.

Someday, I hope, the sport will become more fair, but until that day if you want to be a national competitor you are just going to have to keep playing the game and applying the principles.

How Tournaments Are Structured

Smaller events typically last one full day. They begin in the morning and run through the afternoon. The action is virtually nonstop right through to the finals.

At larger more professional events the action breaks after the afternoon eliminations. The competition resumes later in the evening.

Teaching seminars featuring celebrity instructors are often offered in conjunction with these larger events. Lots of good teaching goes on here, so take advantage of it.

Tournaments normally begin with registration at about 9:00 A.M. By 10:00 A.M. the kata divisions begin, followed soon by fighting.

Hotel discounts and in some cases airline discounts are offered to competitors at many of the major events. Details for each tournament are published in advance on mailers and fliers.

Now that you know what to expect at the typical tournament be aware that tournaments vary quite a bit from place to place. The length of the event depends on its size and the format chosen by the promoter. The actual amount of time the tournament consumes is also greatly affected by the ability of the promoter to run it efficiently and get it over with on time.

Most tournaments, even the biggies, take place in one day. A notable exception is the Internationals, which hosts thousands of competitors and takes a full two days. This mammoth event has approximately 56 divisions between forms and fighting.

The Rules for Fighting

Matches last for two minutes or end when one contestant scores three points. In the event of a tie, there is an overtime period in which one additional point wins the bout. (Time often varies from event to event.)

Safety pads are mandatory in all divisions. Groin protection for males and mouthpieces for all fighters are required at all events. Headgear is usually optional.

Legal targets vary. The common legal targets in point karate tournaments include the head, face, side of the neck, ribs, chest, abdomen, collarbone, groin, and kidneys.

Illegal target areas are the spine, the back of the neck, throat, hip, knee, leg, and feet.

Head butts, hair pulling, bites, open hands, elbows, knees, stomps to the head, jumping on a downed opponent, and blind techniques are normally illegal.

Some events allow sweeping techniques. The sweep itself has no point value. To get a point you must strike a legal target with a legal technique within three seconds of the sweep. The point can be earned by hitting the opponent while he is falling or after he has hit the ground—it does not matter as long as the three-second rule is followed.

At many traditional events, green belts or below will be allowed no head contact. Often in junior divisions and peewee divisions there is no head contact at all. Brown and black belts may have light head contact and black belts may have fairly heavy face and head contact. Keep your eyes open; you can never be too sure what the rules will be.

It is up to you to teach yourself the rules for each tournament you attend. Determine in advance what the duration of the matches will be and what the legal targets for hitting and punching are. Is head contact allowed? Will you lose a point if you step out of bounds?

At some events the value of techniques vary. For example, they may award two points for a kick to the head but only one point for all other legal strikes.

Pay especially close attention to the rules for head contact. At some events you will be able to strike to the side of the head and not to the face. At others head contact may be completely forbidden.

In tournaments in which a strike to the face and head is illegal, points are awarded instead when the punch is pulled. This means that a pulled punch that gets within so many inches of the face and appears to have the velocity and direction to do damage earns a point. The problem with this method is that it is so difficult for the judges to accurately determine what is close enough and powerful enough to gain a point. Who is qualified to determine that a pulled punch would have had the power, range, and focus needed to do real damage?

Rather than depend on the judges to make this nebulous call, I made it my policy to concentrate on contact targets. It was safer to seek a clean shot to the body than to go for a shot using a pulled punch to the head. I would fake to the head to get the opening and then attack the body with enough power to win my point easily.

Disqualifications and Penalties

In the lower belt divisions it is not usually necessary to hit your opponent to score a point. No contact or light contact will usually earn a point, but excessive contact to the face or body may cost you. If the referee determines that you made excessive contact, he may award a penalty point to your opponent. He can call for your disqualification.

A black belt or an instructor who enters the ring uninvited will draw penalty points for his student.

The student might get himself disqualified if he uses foul language or acts in a highly disrespectful manner. Disqualification based on behavior is done at the discretion of the center referee.

How the Divisions Are Split

Divisions are blocked partly in relation to the age of the competitors. Peewee is usually 7 years old and under. Most contests have a division for 8-10 year olds and a group for beginning boys ranging from ages 11-13. There may be a boys advanced division featuring ages 11-13. Boys aged 14-16 usually split into three divisions, one for beginners, one for intermediates, and one for advanced competitors.

There are fewer females at karate tournaments than there are males. The girls division may have only one division for competitors in the ages ranging from 11-14 years. Women 15-16 years and older ranked white to green will compete separately. Women in the same age group with red, brown, and black belts will fall into another division.

For adult males there may be a lightweight division with belt rankings from white to green, a middleweight class with rankings from white to green, and a heavyweight division with rankings from white to green. In the red to brown belt divisions there may be light middleweight fights and heavyweight matches. Among the black belts there is usually a lightweight division (weight 150 pounds and under), a middleweight division (151–175 pounds), and heavyweight (176 and over). Some contests boast a beginning and advanced division for competitors 35 years and older.

Getting Set

There is no rule that requires you to be present for the entire day of a tournament, but it is to your great advantage to be there for the majority of the events. For one thing, divisions seldom begin or end at their assigned times, and although the events will run in sequence it is hard to predict exactly when you will be called to perform.

It is wise to hang around and observe the competition. It is especially important to watch the judges. Make notes in your mind about their preferences. Some will like kicks while others may favor punches. This by no means implies that these fellows are cheating; it simply means that they have favorite techniques. If you know in advance what their pet techniques are, then you can adjust what you are about to do as you get ready to enter the ring. All of this assumes that you are able to determine for sure that the judges you have been watching will indeed be judging your performance (see Chapter 3).

Occasionally the black belt kata division competes first. Promoters often do this to ensure that the black belts will arrive early and therefore be on hand to judge and referee the rest of the divisions as needed.

It is your responsibility as a competitor to hear when your division is called to compete. Do not show up late expecting to jump in. You will not be allowed to compete unless you arrive on time, so keep your ears open.

The Rules for Kata

Divisions

The procedure for the breakdown of divisions and the execution of the contests is more consistent for kata competitions than it is for fighting. This makes your job of learning the rules a bit easier.

The divisions for forms competition in an average tournament break down like this: peewee, ages 11 and under; peewee advanced, 11 years; beginning juniors, age 12–16; advanced juniors, age 12–16; adults ranked from white to green belts, hard style; and adults ranked from white to green belt, soft style. There is a hard-style division that lumps adults with red and brown belts, and a soft-style division that pits adults with red and brown belts against each other.

Normally there is a women's division for black belt women. Women with rankings under the black belt level usually compete with the men in both the hard- and soft-style divisions.

The bigger tournaments have open divisions that allow specialty performances. These may be kata performances put to music or some such special arrangement. In the open competition men and women compete together.

How Kata Is Judged

The method used for judging forms varies somewhat from event to event. As with fighting it is necessary to study the event and the judges in order to conform to the standards of the day.

Turner performs a "soft" style kata.

Part of the complexity results from the fact that hard-style forms and soft-style forms are judged on different criteria. A hard-style kata might be judged, for example, on balance, stance, and focused power. Soft-style forms in the same tournament may be judged on their fluidity of motion, balance, explosiveness, and power.

In my opinion, all forms whether hard or soft in content, should be judged the same. To be effective hard stylists need fluidity and soft stylists need power. Both methods rely on solid stances and contain realistic fighting techniques. Perhaps one day all kata performances will be judged by the same standards, but for now the criteria for judging hard and soft styles is considerably different and generally inconsistent.

The Order of Competition

Statistically it is true that individuals who perform their forms near the beginning of a division get lower average scores than those who compete near the end. This will be a problem only at national tournaments, which easily average between thirty and forty competitors per division.

In order to have their names near the end of the list many forms competitors sign up as late as possible. This late sign-up strategy slows down the process and therefore the entire event. Nowadays some promoters solve this problem by reversing the order of sign-up. In many of today's tournaments the last person to sign up goes first and vice versa.

To make sure that you get signed up as far down on the list as possible talk to the folks handling the sign-up. They are usually quite happy to explain the procedure. Ask them in what order the names will be called and they will tell you. In those rare cases where this information is withheld, try to sign up in the middle of the crowd.

What to Do with Your Free Time

First get yourself registered and determine when you are scheduled to compete. Chances are you will have several hours of free time before your division begins. What should you do?

It has been my experience that most competitors waste the time by socializing with their classmates. The waiting period is traditionally a goof-off period, a time to slap backs and tell jokes.

In my opinion the free time can be used to increase your chances of winning if you put it to good political, psychological, and strategic use.

Check Out the Judges and the Competition

As a competitor I used part of my free time to watch the judges, discerning their habits and their likes and dislikes. I also observed the other competitors. The information you gain by simply watching is invaluable. In addition to learning the quirks and capabilities of the judges and referees, you can find out a great deal about your opponents.

People give away a great deal about themselves by the way they walk, talk, dress, and perhaps most of all by the way they warm up. Surprisingly most competitors warm up with their favorite techniques. Time and time again I am amazed to see top contenders loosening up with their favorite punches and kicks. Many do so with the intention of intimidating their opponents, but they are only giving away part of their fighting strategy. Remember this: Never do your favorite techniques in your warm-up.

Deceptive Warm-Ups

Warm up with things you do not intend to use in the fight. This is a lesson that I learned early in my career—the hard way, I might add. I took it to heart and developed a few very impressive eye-catching techniques to be used exclusively as warm-up maneuvers. I took the time to polish them and to make them look sharp to impress and confuse people who might be watching me. My goal was to get them to worry about a technique that I knew I would never use. When the fighting started my real arsenal came out of the closet.

This strategy is more important at the advanced levels, but it is never too soon to begin developing a deceptive warm-up of your own. Start with a simple strategy. If you know you are going to fight mostly with your feet, warm up with lots of impressive hand techniques. If you intend to fight with your hands, warm up with some flashy kicks.

You will find that your opponents—the good ones—will watch you warm up. They will formulate their strategy partly upon what they see you do as you are getting loose. You will also find that the vast majority of these same folks will continue to warm up with their favorite fighting techniques.

Your deceptive warm-up throws pipes in the spokes of an opponent who has spent his free time watching you warm up. It is a strategy that will work on anyone. I am certain that it would have worked on me. If someone had been warming up in their corner with kicks while planning to fight me with fists, it would have worked on me—my own trick!

Someday you will run into a savvy fighter who makes an effort to trick you by warming up with techniques that he or she will not use in the ring. At least you enter the duel on even ground, both having taken the time to mislead the other. Do not sweat this. You will still have the advantage if your grasp of the principles of winning is complete. The 18 Principles will enable you to quickly determine what type of fighter you are up against.

In summary, remember to use your free time to your advantage. Watch your opponents warm up and memorize or make notes of their favorite techniques. Keep your notepad handy to list the good and bad points of judges and referees.

As the time for your division to compete draws near, you should loosen up—but be careful not to overexert. Warm up with things that you do not intend to use, and make sure that you do these deceptive techniques well.

Politics

Use some of your free time to introduce yourself to the people whom you need to know. Rather than sticking with your buddies, take the time and make the effort to reach out. Introduce yourself to the editors of magazines who have come to cover the event, and shake hands with any martial arts celebrities that happen to be present. Get to know the officials and the tournament's promoter.

I am not suggesting that you brownnose your free time away—just take a moment to introduce yourself. Say, "Hi," and give your name, and then add something like "I want you to know that I have admired you for a long time [if you have!]." Shake hands and go on about your business of observing referees, judges, and your worthy competitors. Make it a point to say hello every time you see that important person after that. After about the fourth hello, he or she will count you as a friend, or at least an acquaintance. Such contacts are invaluable.

Years ago I attended Janiece Miller's Mardigras Tournament in New Orleans. This particular event was the first national tournament that I attended all by myself without my instructor, Al Dacascos.

I was only a gold belt, which gives you an idea of how long ago this was. Traveling halfway across the United States to fight on my own was a big adventure. I was terribly nervous, but of course I did my best not to let it show. At some point during the proceedings a man walked up to me and introduced himself as Al Weiss, the editor of *Official Karate* (the magazine no longer goes by this name). He complimented me on my uniform. I was pleased to meet Al Weiss and flattered by his comment.

When I got back to Denver I received a letter from Weiss. It was probably the nicest professional letter that I ever received during my years as a karate competitor. He wrote, "I just wanted to send you a letter from a jaded old writer to let you know how refreshing it is to see a spark of class on the tournament circuit—the way you dress, the way you act, conduct yourself, the way you look." It made me feel great, and it made me realize how important these things are. I attended that event alone with the low visibility common to all who hold a low belt rank. But because of the way I had presented myself I made an impression on that editor.

Later in my career when I needed publicity I approached him about an article. He was happy to do it and from that time until this day we've been close friends. I keep Al's letter in my scrapbook along with copies of the articles he did for me. This was just one of many valuable friendships and political connections that I was able to make during my tournament career.

Remember to make an effort to introduce yourself to important folks. Shake hands with editors, famous karate fighters and teachers, and of course the judges and referees.

Your Appearance

Dress to Win

John T. Molloy is the author of the famous bestseller *Dress for Success*. Molloy set out to prove to the world that what we wear is, to a large extent, who we are—at least in the eyes of others.

Writes Molloy: "I took two men, both in their thirties, both of average height and weight, and dressed one in lower-middle-class clothes, the other in upper-middle-class apparel. . . . First, the man in upper-middle-class dress stood to the side of a revolving door at the entrance to a building. When he saw someone coming, he attempted to pace his steps so that he and the approaching party would reach the door at exactly the same time. . . . In fifty-eight out of eighty-six attempts, our [well-dressed] man went through first, without any confrontation. . . . When the same test was conducted sixty-two times with our man in lower-middle-class clothes, he was pushed aside more often; and on three separate occasions he was threatened with physical violence."

Molloy undertook dozens of such experiments using hundreds of subjects in a wide array of circumstances. Although his tests were mostly geared toward business attire, his results are universal. Dress like a winner and people will think you are a winner. In the karate world this means dress like a winner and people will treat you with more respect.

By dressing right you can swing opinion in your favor before the competition even starts. Dressing like a winner will also increase your self-image. You will win more when you know that you look good, when you know that you look like a winner.

At some karate events all competitors are required to wear traditional karate or kung fu uniforms. In most cases the rules simply state that the uniforms must be clean and untorn. But in reality a surprising number of competitors present themselves in ragged and unseemly garb. Fewer still take the time to dress like a champion.

How does a champion dress? To get the look of a winner you must spend a little money and develop a uniform with a look that is slightly different from the norm, something that is uniquely yours. I do not mean something flowered, striped, paisley, or fluorescent—I think these radical patterns turn judges off. I mean a nice, crisp, traditional uniform with some subtle difference or quality about it that catches the eye.

All of my competition uniforms are tailored to fit me and complement my body. Unlike store-bought garments, these uniforms fit only me, not everyone in the world who is approximately the same height and weight as I am. When I walked into the ring the lines of my uniform followed and therefore accentuated my movement. My tailored uniforms drew attention to my performance.

My uniforms were designed with a snug fit. They were sewn out of double, two-way-stretch material. Although they were made to form-fit my body, the stretch material gave me all the room I needed to stretch, to move, and to leap.

Custom-made uniforms are a tremendous advantage. Shop around and you will find that it is not too expensive to have a sharp karate

Turner performing in one of her tailored karate uniforms.

uniform made. On the average, I paid about the same for a complete tailor-made outfit as I would have for a store-bought uniform.

Some competitors sharpen up their look by adding a simple stripe down the leg of their store-bought uniform. Anything you can do that makes you stand out without looking silly establishes your trademark. How you look to others may not seem like a big deal to you right now, but just remember that little things make big differences. The little things like clothes and haircuts may be the only difference between a top contender and a champion. The line that separates the best from second best is sometimes razor thin. The champion realizes this and makes every detail work to his advantage.

Your Hairstyle

In addition to your uniform you should pay special attention to your hair. Your hairstyle is part of your winning dress code and an important part of your overall signature. By wearing your hair in a particular style and keeping it in that style all of the time, you make yourself more recognizable. Choose your hairstyle with care and stick to it.

In competition I always wore my hair in a bun. I looked, perhaps, a bit like a schoolteacher and friends teased me about it. But I never, in all my years as a competitor, changed this look. Now people know me by it.

Bowing In

Before you can perform your kata you must bow and introduce yourself and your form. Bow before you enter the ring; approach the officials and bow again. At this point you should introduce yourself, state the name of your form, the name of your school, and perhaps the name of your instructor.

Back up a bit and begin your form. Be sure not to turn your back to the judges, however, as this is considered to be an act of disrespect.

If you are going to execute a form that does not end in exactly the same place that it began, you should inform the judges in advance. Some judges out there think that something is wrong with a kata that does not end in the same place as it started.

By the time you are called upon to perform your kata, you may find that you have been sitting for quite a while. It is perfectly acceptable for you to stand up, bow, and then stretch a little before you begin. Feel free to do it. You do not want to be stiff when you compete. It is dangerous for your muscles and detrimental to your performance.

How Things Work

I long for the day when traditional point karate tournaments become more professional and consistent. That day may be far in the future. At present the rules vary widely from place to place in the United States.

One day, I hope, a governing organization will emerge that will standardize point karate and govern it all across the country. Such an organization will help traditional karate by ensuring that all officials are paid, that clinics for judges and referees are offered, and that officials are required to qualify for the difficult jobs they seek.

When you understand how karate tournaments work you have a tremendous advantage over your rivals. Fewer than 20 percent of competitors have a solid grasp of the rules and know how to read between the lines at a karate event.

A top contender in the karate world is a master of all the details. He knows what kind of events to participate in and which events he needs to win to gain recognition and the necessary points. He has a complete grasp of the inner workings of all the major karate tournaments on the national circuit.

The top contender also knows how to dress for victory, how to play the political game, and how to watch the officials as well as his adversaries. The champion, however, takes this precompetition "science" to an even higher level. He uses body language, verbal and nonverbal signals, and a whole slew of prefight setups. The champion continues to dominate because he uses the 18 Principles of Winning in every phase of his karate life.

8
Bringing Victory Home

J immy Buffet sings: "Living is a pleasure but winning is a treasure that most do not find." It is sad that so many people miss out on the joy of winning. Winning is the best thrill. Once you experience winning you can never be satisfied with losing.

In reality becoming a champion is a simple matter, yet very few people ever do it. The answer to our failures lies in our own lack of ambition and most of all in our inability to see ourselves as winners.

We all know people who lie to themselves about their own abilities and the reasons for their failures. These sad people tell themselves lies so many times that they finally come to believe in the lies themselves.

The rewards of a winner's life are fantastic, and these rewards come only to those who believe in themselves and never give up the fight to achieve their dreams. Every winner I know has gone through struggles and confrontations to achieve their personal victories. None of these champions was "born to win." Behind every champion is a story of personal triumph over obstacles both external and internal.

When you think of yourself as a winner, winning becomes a reality. You are going to become what you think you are. Be aware of what thoughts and self-opinions fill your mind. If you find that your thoughts are filled with self-doubts and sad excuses, then it is time to take control and to reprogram your unconscious with positive self-talk.

*Karyn Turner (right) with
Lena Miller—two winners.*

Mistakes of the Masters

Every competitor makes mistakes. To help you in your struggle to
minimize mistakes, I have listed mistakes made by karate greats. Some
of these were my mistakes, some were made by Bill Wallace, Fred
Wren, Howard Jackson, Jeff Smith, Chuck Norris, Jim Butin, Joe
Lewis, and other karate champions. Here are the nine most common
mistakes.

1. *Overtraining.* For years I trained six hours a day six days a
   week. Finally I realized it was too much. Don't get burned-

out. Do not train too many hours in one day and allow at
least one rest day each week.

2. *Failure to use faking.* Faking is rarely taught in karate
   schools. Take the initiative and learn the art of the fake.

3. *Failure to change rhythm.* If you dance and move to one
   rhythm your opponent will count your steps and use your
   own rhythm to defeat you. Continue to change your rhythm
   all during an exchange.

4. *Showing pain.* When you show pain you tell your opponent
   that you are afraid. Even when you fake pain in order to get a
   point you lose because your opponent will gain confidence.
   You cannot always keep someone from hurting you, but you
   can keep the person from knowing that you hurt.

5. *Failure to use lead-side techniques.* When you use rear-side
   techniques you open yourself to counterattack. Most of your
   attacks should be done with the lead side.

6. *Failure to use footwork.* Footwork keeps you mobile and
   preserves your balance. Mobility is your foundation;
   footwork is your vehicle.

7. *Failure to use the initial move.* I think we should sign a
   petition to get Howard Jackson to come back to the sport
   and teach the initial move. In point competition the initial
   move is by far the most potent tool for success.

8. *Leaning back too far with kicks.* When you lean back with a
   kick you lose the ability to maintain constant forward
   pressure. It is difficult to regain balance after throwing a
   leaning kick and even more difficult to launch a second
   technique.

9. *Relying on only one angle of attack.* Do not give up on your
   favorite techniques. If your opponent is able to block you,
   simply attack him at a different angle. Keep changing angles
   until you get him with your favorite technique.

Every fighter makes mistakes. I certainly made my share. Among the
worst was my tendency, in the early days of my career, to fight without
a plan. Later I was plagued with tension. It was months before I
realized what a mistake I was making by holding my body tight and
rigid while I tried to compete.

Setting Goals

My karate ambition was to become number one. I overcame many challenges and not a few setbacks in my struggle to attain this goal. I achieved my goal in a relatively short period of time because I had desire and because I did not hit any insurmountable obstacles. Often I have wondered what would have happened to my ambition if I had come up against a situation that I could not overcome.

The Howard Jackson Story

Howard Jackson was faced with a setback that wrecked his point tournament career just at the moment he was realizing his goal to be recognized as the very best point karate fighter in the country.

"*Black Belt* magazine and several other publications had just acknowledged me as number one," Jackson said. "*Official Karate* magazine said I would be number one for years to come unless angels from heaven descended and took it away from me."

Jackson was considered to be the best of the best with a brilliant future ahead when tragedy struck. "I had trained hard to be the best," related Jackson, shaking his head. "I'd been working with Chuck Norris and Joe Lewis. I felt that I was far ahead of everyone else."

Jackson won fight after fight by a spread of 3–0 on the day his goal to be the best came to a screeching halt. "It was like the Howard Jackson show that day," he said. The next and last opponent Jackson would fight on that fateful day was no different from the rest. "Everything I threw landed," he said. "I was having a good time. I jumped into the air and kicked the guy right in the head. I landed on my left leg and spun to throw a heelkick/roundhouse combination. Suddenly my knee collapsed underneath me. I was lying on the floor in pain. I didn't know it yet but the cartilage in my knee was badly torn."

The "angel" that struck Jackson down was a little devil sitting ringside. "As I lay on the floor I realized that I had slipped on a paper cup," he said. "A fan had thrown a paper cup into the ring, presumably at me."

Jackson's next fight would have been against Benny ("the Jet") Urquidez. "He and I had been rivals for years," Jackson said. "I looked forward to fighting him. He ended up winning the grand championship I felt would have been mine."

What irony to have karate's number-one ranked fighter knocked out of his dream of becoming grand champion by something as trivial as

Karyn Turner and Lena Miller demonstrate the Chinese chain, one of Turner's favorite weapons.

a paper cup. Yet Jackson's doctors explained that the damage would almost surely require surgery.

"I found one doctor who thought it might be possible to rehabilitate my knee with exercise. I tried it and even entered a tournament." It was the first world full contact karate match in the United States. He fought with his damaged knee tightly wrapped. His loss marked the first time he had been defeated since his early days as a tournament fighter.

"I made up my mind to have surgery and did," he said. It took many long months for Jackson's knee to recover its strength. When he finally returned to the karate circuit, the whole karate scene had changed. Point karate was no longer squarely in the limelight. Jackson realized that he had missed his chance to become a famous karate personality. The narrow window of stardom closed during the months of his recuperation.

But Jackson saw the whole episode as an opportunity. "My physical and mental comeback showed me what I could do mentally," he said.

Karate great Howard Jackson and Chuck Martinez make announcements at a 1979 event.

After recovering from the mishap Jackson kept struggling until he eventually became a world champion in full contact karate. Later he earned the title of world champion in international style kickboxing in competition against the Japanese and the Thais. Still it was not enough for Jackson.

"I became number six in the world in professional boxing. I covered a lot of ground just to show myself that I could overcome the obstacle of injury and pain. The comeback was a challenge," Jackson said.

Why was Howard Jackson able to rise from the ashes of his unfortunate injury at the turning point of his career? Like most winners Jackson set goals. "Everything I set my mind to I hold strong until I achieve what I set out to do no matter how long it takes," he said. His goal to be a champion was the simple theme that fueled his comeback and his subsequent success.

Setting Your Theme Goal

Without a theme goal it is unlikely that you will ever become a karate champion. There are many distractions on the long road to the top. The only sure way to arrive is to proceed along your journey with a clearly marked map. Your theme goal is your mission statement; it is your map for success.

No one can set goals for another, but seeing how others plan for their success may help you as you map your own future. To keep it simple let's imagine that you are a competent martial artist with solid mechanical skills and that you are just getting started in a point karate career.

Your first task is to put your long-range goal (theme goal) into a short and clear statement. Your long-range goal might read something like this: **"I, (insert your name), am (becoming) the number one fighting and forms competitor in the United States."**

Notice how I wrote the goal in the present tense? This is important as your unconscious mind does not distinguish future state from present state very well. Stating and reciting your goal in the present tense has a more potent effect.

Experts tell us that if you state your goal with your name inserted, it is more effective than a goal stated with a pronoun only. Each time you state your goal your unconscious hears it and hears your name with it.

Some say the process of planting a goal in the unconscious is like programming a computer. Perhaps it is even more like training a dog—repetition, repetition, and repetition—that is what works.

Your theme goal is your lighthouse in the storm of training. All of your short-term, mid-term, and long-term objectives will be guided by your simple and concise statement of your theme goal. I recommend that you write it or type it onto several three-by-five cards and tape them in conspicuous places, such as on your bathroom mirror, on your bedpost, over your heavy bag, and on the dashboard of your car. Repeat your theme goal daily and never, never neglect its power and influence on your future.

Short-Term Goals and Objectives

From unknown to best known is a big jump, and the job of becoming number one in your karate class may seem too big to tackle. Achievement of such a lofty goal takes a lot of work but it need not be overwhelming.

Treat your ultimate goal as you might a Thanksgiving turkey. Do not try to eat the whole thing at one meal. Get your pencil out and split your long-range objective into two parts—level one and level two. Then break them down even further into months, weeks, days, and hours.

It is entirely realistic for you to become a widely recognized regional competitor within the span of one year. By the end of your second year you could be a national champion. At the end of your third year you could be number one in the country. Four or five years from now you could be an internationally known martial artist and champion. It is possible and it all begins with your daily workout.

Working to Achieve Your Goal

Daily Routine

Establish a training routine and stick with it. Your workouts should include running and other aerobic exercises to build up wind and stamina, sparring, heavy-bag training, shadowboxing, focus-mitt training, kata training, light-weight training, and technique training.

Include mental training in your daily routine. Positive self-talk and

Turner demonstrates perfect form with her Chinese double swords.

other attitude-adjusting exercises should be a part of everything you do.

Establish a timetable for your workouts and stick to it. You body will become regulated to the pattern that you set and working out will get easier. For example, you might design your day to include running and aerobics in the early morning, sparring and bag work in the early evening, and weight training afterwards. Although the intensity of your workouts will vary between hard days, long days, and easy days, you will still hold to the basic time pattern.

Vary your workout to avoid burnout. Get different sparring partners when possible and add new elements to your regime from time to time.

I cannot overstate the importance of eating right and getting plenty of sleep. Your body must have fuel and rest in order to achieve its greatest gains.

Weekly Recap

Tracking your own progress is much like trying to see your own child grow. Day by day you will notice nothing, but when grandmother comes to visit she cannot get over how much your little one has grown. Even rapid progress in the martial arts feels slow. Without some way to monitor the gradual changes that your body is going through you may become frustrated with training. Therefore it is essential that you track yourself each week.

Dedicate a notebook or use your computer to log your training time. You should make entries each day and do a summary at the end of each week that answers the following questions.

1. How many hours did I invest in running, sparring, heavy-bag training, shadowboxing, focus-mitt training, stretching, kata training, light-weight training, and technique training?
2. What and how much positive self-image and self-confidence building did I do?
3. How many class hours did I log?
4. How many hours of sleep did I average per night?
5. What and how much did I eat?

You must look back each week and log the statistics of your training and evaluate your progress or you will soon lose sight of your goals. Writing or recording the information keeps you on track and gives you a journal that acts as a growth chart. In six months you can look back and see in writing exactly how much time and work you have invested. You will also be able to see just how much you have grown as a martial artist.

Objectives for the First Year

Before you begin your first year as a regional competitor in the open tournament circuit, you should amass considerable experience in closed tournaments and local tournaments. Be certain that your grasp of the mechanics of your system is intact. It is also necessary that you save some expense money before embarking on your first year in the regional circuit.

This first year is the time to test the 18 Principles of Winning and to find the rank level at which you should compete. In the regional circuit you will gain a high level of experience without spending excessive amounts of money.

Compete as often as possible but do not neglect your training. Go to karate classes regularly and make it a point to attend every seminar that you can, providing that the instructor is a skilled martial artist with experience and expertise in tournament karate.

Never fear working out with or learning from individuals whom you may later be competing against. Sparring with people whom you know forces you to rely on the principles rather than just on technique. You have the basics of your root style well in hand, and it is time to borrow from other styles.

Study martial arts publications during the entire first year. Read everything you can find that lists ratings and compares the virtues of various fighters and tournaments.

Learn about the sanctioning organizations, and get an overview of the rules used by each group at all major tournaments. Talk to competitors about the national circuit. Gain as many friends from the national circuit as possible. Outline your strategy for your second year. Put away as much travel money as you can.

Midway through your first year or whenever you achieve a level of recognition, go ahead and develop a press release. Collect black-and-white photographs of yourself in action. Hire a photographer to shoot if necessary, but get some good shots and send them in to the magazines that publish ratings. As they say about the business world, "You have to toot your own horn."

Make it your strategy to get your photographs and press release into the hands of as many publications and as many influential people as you can. Promoting yourself successfully at the regional level is a must to get started right on the national beat.

At any time during the first year that you feel that you are ready for the national circuit, cut loose and go for it. You will know when you are ready for the big time.

Shortly before you get ready for your push into the national level of competition, engage the services of a good writer who is familiar with the martial arts or other sports. Place some articles in the martial arts magazines and spread your name around a bit.

The Second Year and Beyond

Assuming that everything has gone smoothly for you during your first year as a serious regional karate contender, you may wish to enter national competition. This is the big time, and success at this level is tough to achieve. You will face three major challenges when you enter this level: tough competitors, the battle for national media coverage; and meeting your expenses.

Since you have the 18 Principles you will find that the tough competitors on the national circuit are manageable. Fighting these people will seem easy compared to the struggles you will face in gaining media coverage and in covering your expenses.

Appear in public and promote yourself as often as possible. Get publicity in any legitimate and tasteful way that you can. Several fighters I know got noticed by riding the coattails of famous martial artists. If, for example, a famous martial artist like Bill Wallace announced that he would be teaching a local seminar, these fighters would call him on the phone before the event. After introducing themselves these enterprising folks would offer to be a free training dummy and demonstration opponent for the duration of the seminar.

Surprisingly they were almost never turned down when they made this offer to work free. Imagine the reputation you could gain if you became known among your peers as Bill Wallace's training second?

The benefits work both ways—letting you be his teaching dummy saves the celebrity teacher a bundle of money and cuts away one of his largest headaches. Few national seminar instructors make advanced arrangements regarding their demonstration partners.

Also offer to be the interview partner for any television spots or interviews that your celebrity seminar teacher is asked to do. What better way to learn martial arts, help another martial artist, and promote yourself?

When you go national it is time to turn up the heat on your self-promotion strategy. Along with your press release and photograph for national publications begin sending letters about your accomplishments to international schools.

Cutting Costs on the National Circuit

Unless you are filthy rich you probably will not be able to make as many national tournaments as you would like. Since you know that you cannot go to every tournament, you may wish to write a budget to include as many of the important tournaments as possible.

One strategy is to spend the money to hit only the largest of the large tournaments. These A-rated events have bigger prizes and offer more points to the competitors who win their events. A few wins at these premium events are worth considerably more than the points that would be earned at the same number of smaller tournaments.

A second strategy is to avoid the high-profile tournaments in favor of smaller events. In order to earn points fast the best competitors will be hitting the A-rated tournaments while avoiding the B- and C-rated events. This means that you will face less competition at the smaller contests.

If you can attend enough B and C tournaments, you may find that you can win your points without spending as much on entry fees and travel while at the same time avoiding much of the toughest competition. Meanwhile you gain lots of experience to get ready for major competition on the national circuit.

When you feel that you are ready and you hunger for the bigger prizes and trophies of the A-rated events, you may still face money problems. Fortunately, by this time, you will be an experienced veteran tournament competitor and your knowledge will be very valuable to other competitors. You can cut your costs by offering to teach seminars at national and international tournaments.

Begin by sending information about yourself to schools. Include a cover letter stating your qualifications and your goals. Enclose your press release each time and be sure to add any demonstration and teaching experience you have.

My Hard Knocks demonstration team became world famous, but in

Karyn Turner's Hard Knocks team shows off various weapons used in performance.

the beginning I formed it as a way to cut costs. I was lucky because I had money to travel and compete, but many of my fellow martial artists were unable to attend the events they needed to be at in order to advance their careers.

To my delight the demonstration team concept worked very well to help defray the costs of tournament participation. My team was able to travel all over the country because the promoters paid our expenses. Through word of mouth we quickly gained popularity and soon The Hard Knocks were in high demand.

The Hard Knocks team was so successful that we ended up touring many countries and performing at every major martial arts event in the world. Think about forming or joining a demonstration team. It is a wonderful way to cut costs and at the same time increase your visibility in the tournament community.

Becoming a Champion: What to Expect

It may happen at the end of your second year or perhaps at the end of your fifth year as a competitor—but it will happen. Providing that you have at least average physical ability and providing that you apply the 18 Principles of Winning and do the things you have learned in this book, you will become a karate champion.

When you win at karate you become more than a good karate practitioner—you become a winner. When you are a winner in karate you are a winner in life. Once cultivated, the competitive spirit will live inside you for the rest of your life.

Vince Lombardi said, "Winning isn't everything; it is the only thing." When we win often enough we become winners in our hearts. Winning increases our confidence and boosts our ability to overcome obstacles.

Continuous Karate Achievement

In the course of my tournament career I realized all of my karate dreams. I won tournament after tournament and grew famous as a karate entertainer. For years I have earned a living from the skills and notoriety of my karate experience.

After all these years and all of this success, I realize now that my ultimate karate achievement did not occur when I won the Grand Championship in both forms and fighting in the same year at Ed Parker's Internationals Tournament. It did not happen when I led The Hard Knocks team through a flawless demonstration of karate skills on national television or in front of the Duke and Duchess of Windsor. The greatest achievement of all is yet to happen.

It may come when I produce a karate competitor far superior to myself and see him or her succeed as a world-class champion, or it may happen when I achieve my highest objectives as a karate promoter. The point is this: karate is a lifetime endeavor. The goals just keep getting higher. Each time a goal is met a new and broader goal takes its place.

A Career in Karate

A championship title is like a diploma in the world of karate careers. The idea that I would work in the field of karate was always in the back of my mind during my karate tournament days. I sought publicity and garnered recognition with the intention that I could someday earn an income with the sport. It worked for me, and I have made my living as a karate promoter for many years.

If you love karate as much as I do, there is no reason why you cannot become a professional martial arts instructor, or a full contact karate trainer. With the popularity of a national karate champion you could end up with a related career in acting, advertising, or promoting. You could easily make all or part of your living by working the seminar circuit like Bill Wallace, Dan Inosanto, and Joe Lewis.

The Final Secrets of Winning

A winner never really loses because he sees each contest as a stepping-stone to his long-range goal of becoming a champion. If his opponent outscores him today, he simply learns from his mistakes and uses the information to win later. With each battle the winner learns more about his competition and more about his own strengths and weaknesses.

Becoming a winner is a process of becoming a master of yourself. To become a winner you must confront and overcome all of your weaknesses. Through this long and difficult process you will find yourself.

Understanding yourself, your abilities, your limitations, and your worth is the final trophy of your martial arts career. Competition is the master key that unlocks all of the riches inside you.

There is a demon that plagues many potential karate champions—procrastination. This condition is very serious. The only known cure is a two-step process: 1. Just do it. If you want to become a champion you must start today on some level—you must do something today. Tomorrow you can make your long-range plans and goals, but today you must do something to start. 2. No matter what happens, keep doing it. Stick with your plan every single day.

The world is full of starters but it has few finishers. The majority of karate competitors are too anxious. They give up at the first sign of difficulty or after their first taste of defeat. Start training for competition today and stay with it everyday. You will succeed.

Glossary

Angles of attack. Various possible angles from which one may attack an opponent. (See Principle 17 in Chapter 1.)

Arnis sticks. Bamboo sticks from martial arts of the Philippines.

Awards. Trophies and cash given to the winners of various divisions in tournaments.

Backkick. One of the five primary techniques. (See Chapter 4.)

Backward runner. A fighter who constantly backs away from his opponent.

Belt divisions. Belt divisions vary from tournament to tournament and from style to style. Some common ones are: black belt, brown belt, blue belt, gold belt, green belt, orange belt, and white belt.

Black belt. The highest ranking in karate; often associated with the level at which one may teach.

Blocker. A fighter who relies heavily on a block-and-counter fighting style.

Body language. The information exchanged between persons on a nonverbal level. This includes both intentional and nonintentional communication.

Broken rhythm. Various tempos and rhythms used to confuse an opponent.

Butterfly sword. A short sword with a curved hand guard that completely covers the fist. This Chinese weapon is used in pairs.

Chain. A whip made of metal, which comes in various lengths.

Chamber. To cock an arm or leg back before striking.

Champion. One who consistently wins at tournament karate and rises to the top of the ratings.

Charger. A fighter who attacks first (also called a jammer). The charger prefers to rush an opponent and hates to retreat.

Chinese animal systems. Tiger, crane, snake, preying mantis—a whole zooful of systems make up this wide category. These styles are complex methods of fighting with forms that are rich with elegant postures.

Chinese broad sword. The Chinese broad sword has a thick blade that is sharp on one side. The weapon curves slightly and is used primarily for slicing.

Chinese double swords. Two swords that fit together inside one sheath. They are shaped like but are lighter than the broad sword.

Chinese hooked swords. Chinese swords, used in pairs, with curved tips and half-moon hand guards, which are sharp. The sword blade is sharp on both sides, and the base of the weapon is sharp and pointed.

Chinese kenpo. A system made popular by Ed Parker; said to be the first Chinese system taught publicly in the United States.

Choy Li Fut. Chinese system with northern and southern influences.

Confidence borrowing. The act of mentally borrowing confidence from one area of your life to help you feel more confident in another area.

Creating an opening. Any variety of techniques and strategies used to cause an opponent to lower his guard.

Creeping footwork. A method of moving closer to an opponent in tiny steps to sneak into striking range.

Critical-distance line. The point at which an opponent can be reached with a punch or kick.

Diamond Nationals Tournament. An important A-rated tournament held in Minnesota. The only tournament that awards diamonds to the winners of certain events.

Division. A category in which a fighter competes.

Dojo. Japanese for training hall.

Dojang. Korean for training hall.

Double-edged long sword. A long straight sword that is sharp on both sides.

Double hyperextension. The reach you gain when you skip or hop forward and then slide forward as you extend your technique.

Dress code. The rules for dress at a tournament; rules vary from event to event.

Elongating movements. The stretching of stances and broadening of postures in order to create a more theatrical and graphic presentation of kata.

Elusive runner. A fighter who evades by running here and there in unpredictable patterns.

Five primary techniques. Bruce Lee identified the following five techniques as primary: the backfist, the reverse punch, the sidekick, the backkick, and the roundkick.

Foot pads. Pads worn on the feet during point karate fights. They cover the top and sides of the feet but leave the bottoms of the feet bare.

Form. A kata, a choreographed sequence of karate movements.

Four types of fighters. The charger, the runner, the blocker, and the elusive runner.

Frontkick. A straight kick that hits with the ball of the foot or the heel.

Full contact karate. The sport of kickboxing.

Gi. Japanese for karate uniform.

Goju-ryu. One of the four most popular Japanese karate systems.

Groin kick. A kick to the genitals; illegal in most tournaments.

Half-commitment. Acting in a way that causes an opponent to expect you to do something that you are not going to do.

Hand pads. Protective hand covers used in point karate.

Hapkido. A Korean system noted for its extensive use of kicks. Hapkido has no traditional kata, but its techniques are well suited for creative competition kata construction.

Hard style. A martial art that relies heavily on power movements.

Headgear. Face and head protection for karate training.

Heavyweight. The heaviest division in karate competition.

Hook. A circular punch common to boxing and kickboxing, similar to karate ridgehand.

Hookkick. A circular kick that strikes with the heel.

Hyperextension. The extra reach you get by sliding forward as you execute a maneuver.

Initial move. The first strike in a series of strikes. (See Principle 4 in Chapter 1.)

Internationals Tournament. The granddaddy of all karate tournaments and karate's largest annual event. Sponsored by Ed Parker, it takes place each year in California.

Intimidation. A strategy used to scare an opponent out of doing his best.

Isshin-ryu. An Okinawan karate style.

Jab. A straight punch from the lead hand. This technique is more common to boxers and kickboxers than to point karate fighters.

Jammer. A fighter who rushes his opponents and attempts to land a first strike (also called a charger).

Jump-spinning backkick. A turning backkick done in the air.

Juniors. A karate tournament division for youngsters.

Kali sticks. Two short sticks usually made of strong bamboo. Kali is an art of the Philippines.

Kama. A small sickle attached to the end of a short stick. This weapon originated in Okinawa. Practitioners of modern karate often employ two kama at one time.

Karate. A Japanese martial art. In the United States the term karate often refers to all types of martial arts.

Karateka. One who practices karate.

Kata. Japanese for form or set. Kata has also become a generic term and refers to any choreographed sequence of martial arts moves regardless of the style.

Kiai. Refers to the shout given by karate fighters to boost their own confidence while striking fear into their opponent.

Kickboxing. The sport of full contact karate. Kickboxing is a term also used by the fighters of Thailand who fight with very different rules from Americans.

Kung fu. A term that has evolved to mean all types of Chinese martial arts.

Kwoon. Chinese for training hall.

Leading centers. Exposing the center of the body.

Leg kick. A kick to the thigh. This kick is illegal in point karate.

Legal targets. The body zones that can be struck in a karate tournament. Striking legal targets earns points; targets vary from tournament to tournament.

Light contact. Fighting with minimal power.

Lightweight. A division for lighter fighters.

Line. The line at which fighters face each other before engaging in combat.

Long spear. A long stick topped with a pointed blade. Spears come in many lengths and are often adorned with colorful tassels.

Long staff. A wooden rod usually about six feet in length. Practitioners select longer or shorter staffs to suit their build.

Mouthpiece. A plastic guard worn to protect the teeth during karate bouts.

Nunchaku. Two sticks attached by a short chain or rope. Originally the nunchaku was used by Okinawan farmers to flail grain.

Nunte. A short swordlike weapon, similar to a sai except that one of the arched prongs curves away from the hand and one curves toward the hand.

Official. A judge or referee at a karate tournament.

Okinawa karate. Karate from Okinawa.

Open circuit. Tournaments open to all styles.

Open division. A special division allowing a wide variety of karate performances, some with music.

Overhand right. A boxing term that refers to a punch similar to the karate reverse punch.

Peewees. The division for the youngest competitors in a karate tournament.

Point. A value given to a hit upon a legal target in a karate tournament.

Point circuit. Tournaments that participate in regional and national karate ratings.

Preform form. A series of flashy movements done before the competitor begins a kata. The purpose is to gain the attention of the judges and the audience.

Press release. A karate press release usually includes biographical information, tournament statistics, and a photograph.

Pulled punch. A punch that is retracted before it hits.

Quando. A heavy staff topped with a large curved blade. A heavy, pointed spearhead is on the other end as a means of balancing this weapon.

Rank. A karate belt rank, such as black belt, green belt, or white belt.

Rating system. A system used by an organization to rate karate competitors on a regional or national level.

Referee. An individual who stands on the floor during a bout and administers official calls.

Relaxation. One of the great secrets of karate power.

Reverse punch. A punch that travels across the body in order to deliver the full power of the hip into the strike. The reverse punch is one of the five primary techniques and is similar to the boxer's jab.

Right cross. A punch used by boxers and kickboxers, similar to the reverse punch of traditional karate.

Ring. A roped-off area for karate competition. The ring also describes the open area in which point fighters compete.

Roundkick. A kick that circles and strikes with the instep or the ball of the foot. The roundkick is one of the five primary techniques of karate.

Safety equipment. Hand, foot, groin, mouth, and chest protection worn by karate fighters.

Sai. A short swordlike weapon. It has two curved prongs that act as a hand guard and a sword catcher.

Samurai sword. A long, curved sword from Japan, sharp on one side. Hilts protect the handle, and the handle is long enough to allow for a two-handed grip.

Self-tale. Positive self-programming statements.

Sex divisions. Divisions that separate men and women at karate tournaments.

Shaolin. A temple in China and a term referring to hard-style martial arts from China.

Shito-ryu. A major karate system, said to have originated in Okinawa and found its way to Japan.

Shotokan. One of four major Japanese karate systems.

Sidekick. A straight kick using the full power of the hips. The strike is made with the heel or the side of the foot.

Soft style. Any martial arts that uses many fluid and relaxed movements.

Stance. A fighting posture.

Street fight. A fight with no rules.

Tae kwon do. A hard-style Korean system.

Telegraphing. Giving away your intentions.

Thai boxing. Kickboxing from Thailand that allows elbow and knee strikes and kicking to the legs and groin. This sport is seldom seen inside the United States.

Three-sectional staff. Three short pieces of staff linked together with rope or chain. This weapon is of Chinese origin.

Tonfa. A short, thick piece of wood with a handle. It is thought to be derived from a tool used by Okinawan farmers or millers.

Tournament. A formal karate competition.

Tournament rating. Tournaments are rated A, B, or C. Points earned at an A-rated event have more value than those from a C- or B-rated tournament.

Uniform. The garb of a karate practitioner.

Uppercut. A rising punch used primarily by kickboxers and boxers.

Wado-ryu. One of the four major Japanese karate styles.

Warning. A condition cited by a referee against a fighter who violates a rule.

White belt. Beginners in the martial arts.

Wu shu. A modern form of Chinese martial arts in which students practice a mixture of traditional and nontraditional maneuvers.

Index

Page numbers in italics refer to photographs.